INTRODUCTION

I'd like to say I wrote this book simply because hot dogs are my all-time favorite food and leave it at that. They are, after all. However, that would leave this page awfully blank. So here is my attempt at describing just how obsessed I am with hot dogs, and why you should be, too.

For me, the story starts about 20 years ago, around the time of my earliest memories and around the age at which I, a typical American child, was introduced to the magic that is American fare: those quick, not-so-healthy but oh-so-delicious foods—pizza, cheeseburgers, tacos, and, of course, hot dogs. My first hot dog was a Plain Jane on a boring bun topped with nothing more than a squirt of mustard and possibly a little ketchup—don't judge me. I was 7. Despite the unimaginative toppings of that first wiener, it was love at first bite. I remember countless birthdays centered on glorious stacks of frankfurters. I insisted that our weekly grilled meals contain plenty of the tube-shaped meat to go around. And when I eventually learned how to cook on my own, at the spoiled age of 15, I made one thing and one thing only: hot dogs.

In high school, friends were amazed at my ability to consume hot dogs every day for months. The lunch lady knew me by name and made sure to set aside a few extra links for me in case they ran out. In college, my nicknames began to reflect my love of this meaty, bread-heavy, topping-laden snack. Even though I knew how to cook, and cook well at that, I prepared hot dogs for special nights in, and I dragged weary dates to hot dog stands for anniversaries or special occasions. But my friends soon resented my obsession with the weenie. As the semesters piled on, I was no longer asked where we should go to lunch; my friends conveniently chose for me, and the hot-dog-filled stands and diners I once dragged us to disappeared from our repertoire.

You see, what I knew (and what my friends *didn't* know) is that the hot dog can be different every time you take a bite. Where they ordered the same toppings on the same bun with the same weenie over and over, I explored the vast, varied world of wienerdom. They thought hot dogs were tired. I knew they were alive with possibilities.

These days, when I mention red hots, frankfurters, foot-longs, hotshots, tube dogs, or dachshund sandwiches, my friends take notice. Their ears perk up and their stomachs rumble. Because now they know that when I say *hot dog*, I mean *haute dog*. They know to expect a trip down a back alley where, hidden between an abandoned warehouse and a dive bar, sits a decades-old diner that serves the most marvelous, topping-heavy, plump and juicy dogs around. Or they know to expect an expensive visit to some upscale and trendy bistro where the hot dog has been redefined from street food to black-tie fare. And they know that the next time we go for hot dogs, they'll be biting into something completely different, a dog they've never tried before.

That's what haute dogs are. They aren't the same old tired dog you've been eating in your backyard since you were a kid. Haute dogs are the edible manifestation of the world's love for this time-tested meal in a bun and the culmination of over a century of culinary creativity. Haute dogs can be found in just about every town and every country. Chances are everyone has tried one at some point—and deciding who makes the best local haute dog can be as divisive as ranking hometown sports teams. You can find haute dogs in street carts, at food trucks, in diners, delis, bistros, and restaurants, and you can make them in your kitchen or out in your backyard, too.

Today, haute dogs are popping up on every continent (okay, except maybe Antarctica, but I bet someone is working on that). So what happens when you take an American fast-food classic and combine it with regional cuisine, deluxe ingredients, secret recipes, and cultural idiosyncrasies? You get sloppy chili dogs, chunky chutney dogs, and dogs fried in the middle of a waffle. You get dogs slathered in rémoulade, buried in French fries, and smeared with homemade ketchup—or no ketchup at all. You get haute dogs . . . and you get this book.

RUSSELL VAN KRAAYENBURG

HAUTE DOGS

RECIPES FOR DELICIOUS
HOT DOGS, BUNS, AND CONDIMENTS

QUIRK
BOOKS

TO MY MOTHER,

LOREE VAN KRAAYENBURG,

WHO ALWAYS TAUGHT ME TO EAT MY VEGETABLES.

I PUT VEGETABLES ON SOME OF THESE DOGS.

DOES THAT COUNT?

Library of Congress Cataloging in Publication Number: 2013911675

ISBN: 978-1-59474-675-8

Printed in China
Typeset in Chronicle and Neutra
Designed by Amanda Richmond
Production management by John J. McGurk

Quirk Books
215 Church St.
Philadelphia, PA 19106
quirkbooks.com

10 9 8 7 6 5 4 3 2 1

CONTENTS

HISTORY: WHICH CAME FIRST— THE BUN OR THE DOG?

I hate when history books start with "as with many things, the true origins here are unknown" but unfortunately, as with many foods, the true origins of the hot dog *are* unknown.

Although it would be nice to point to one sweeping, cinematic story of how the hot dog came to be, chances are it took shape in many places at once, growing out of a long-lasting love of both the sausage and the bread. Somewhere in the millennia-long history of these two staples, people began putting the two together, and sometime after that an American classic, one that would spread over the entire world within one short century, was born.

Instead of cute folktales about how the bun saved vendors the annoyance of customers stealing the customary gloves used to serve naked sausages, or how an inventive baseball stadium ice-cream vendor invented the bun-wrapped sausage to see his business through a cold-weather slump, I'll tell you the truth. Somewhere in history, some enterprising foodie added that convenient slice down the center of the bun that turns an otherwise unassuming loaf of bread into the perfect, portable vessel for a piping hot frankfurter.

Bread can be traced back to the beginnings of civilization, when humans shifted from hunters and gathers to farmers. Sometime around 7000 BC, early farmers in the fertile crescent of Mesopotamia (modern-day Iran and Syria) domesticated wheatlike crops whose grains would become a sine qua non for breadmaking, and the first professional breadmakers turned up around 2000 BC. Ancient Egyptians are thought to have discovered—accidentally—that the natural yeasts found in the air could be used to leaven bread when some forgetful chef left out dough overnight. But flat, tough, utilitarian loaves still ruled the first dozen or so centuries of bread—the Romans believed unleavened bread was healthier. Two important developments came when ancient Romans began to use wind power to grind finer flours and "borrow" from European tribes the technique of leavening bread with brewer's yeast (elsewhere, chunks of dough from the previous day's baking would be added to leaven breads).

By the Middle Ages bread had become a staple for most and a lavish luxury for others; in fact, the English words *lord* and *lady* are derived from the Old English for "keeper of the loaf" and "kneader of the loaf." By 1886, writer H. L. Mencken was already penning complaints about the "soggy rolls prevailing today" in the world of sausage sandwiches, and a 1904 obituary in the *Brooklyn Daily Times* mourned the death of one Ignatz Fischmann, a baker credited with the invention of so-called milk rolls for holding hot dogs. Although the word *bun* (from a French word for "swelling," describing the bulbous shape of the bread) had been in use

since the 15th century, it didn't show up in conjunction with *hot dog* until sometime in the 1920s, when it seems to have edged out *roll* as the moniker of choice for an oblong, sliced bread product. The modern era for bread came in 1928 with the popularization of presliced bread, which changed how the world looked at loaves of bread (and was the best thing since, well, ever). Seven years later, Mary Ann Baking Company in Chicago introduced a high-gluten, poppy-seed-studded bun with a sturdier texture designed to hold up to steaming—one of the first regional innovations in dog design.

Sausages have been around for nearly as long as bread. Originally used to preserve meat for storing as animal husbandry grew, the humble sausage quickly turned from utilitarian solution to art as butchers began adding spices and herbs to improve flavor. Ancient civilizations regularly prepared, cured, and smoked sausages—they're even mentioned in Homer's *Odyssey*—but it wasn't only Europe where sausage was popular. Accounts of various cured, packed meats spring up in China as early as in Europe and North Africa. Sausages continued to

HOT DOGS IN HISTORY: CRAZY ABOUT HOT DOGS

A 7th-century text known as *Symeon the Holy Fool* may contain the earliest known description of a hot dog fanatic: a man who wore a string of sausages around his neck and "smeared mustard on the mouths of some of those who came to joke with him."

grow in popularity through the Middle Ages, especially in colder countries like Germany and Austria, where their utility as hardy, storage-friendly fare came in handy. Sausage making was a necessity for getting valuable meat to survive the winter months when fewer fruits, vegetables, and grains were available. These old-world sausages consisted of a hand-made mixture of meat, fat, and spices that had a coarse texture. Modern sausage and hot dog making, like sliced bread, came after the invention of the hot dog. For years, hot dogs were made with butcher-made frankfurters and wieners. Named for the German city of Frankfurt, frankfurters or franks were typically made of various combinations of lean pork, bacon fat, and sometimes ingredients like pig heart and tripe. In 1904, German butcher Johann Georg Lahner took his frank-making operation to a new frontier in Vienna (Wien in German), where his pork-and-beef riff on the smoked sausage became known as a *wiener*. Today, hot dogs are prepared efficiently and almost automatically by specialized machines. Meat is chopped and ground, mixed with additives, fillers, or flavoring agents, and then further ground into a fine-textured paste to be stuffed into casings. The stuffed dogs are smoked and then cooled, peeled, packaged, and sealed for shipping.

So sausages and bread have existed side by side for centuries, but when were they first put together—and by whom? Sausages and rolls are served together in Germany, though rarely in hot dog form; elsewhere in Europe, the sausage often lived on its own perhaps on the same plate as bread but not inside it. Most accounts attribute the eventual marriage of bread and tubular meat to late-19th-century America, when immigrants brought frankfurters to the States. There they were popularized by such legendary vendors as A. L. Feuchtwanger of St. Louis and Charles Feltman of Coney Island—one (or both) of whom pioneered the dog-in-bun idea. More than likely, the long, soft, white rolls sprang up in multiple locations, the brainchild of more than one enterprising local baker. In 1916, Nathan Handwerker's iconic stand on Coney Island opened its doors.

A NATHAN-AL TREASURE

The first Nathan's Fourth of July Hot Dog Eating Contest was held in 1916 and has been canceled only twice since then: in 1941, to protest the war in Europe, and again in 1971, to protest civil unrest and the reign of free love.

Toppings were latecomers to the game. Like other hot dog components, mustard seeds have been cultivated since at least the days of ancient Greece. The condiment flourished in medieval times—many castles even employed a *mustardarius*, a servant devoted exclusively to preparing and serving mustard. Commercial mustard took off in Dijon, France, around the 14th century, with Germany and England also developing their own distinctive flavors and strengths. Historically, the term *relish* is something of a catchall to refer to any kind of condiment, but the variety of pickled vegetables we've come to know is probably of English origin.

True to this European pedigree, the first dogs in the United States were topped with some combination of mustard or relish (Mencken, ever the eager hot-dog killjoy, described hot dog mustard as "flabby" and "puerile"). But as the 19th century came to a close and a new century burgeoned, the toppings found on street-cart and diner hot dogs began reflecting the tastes of the new immigrants who sold them as well as the communities they catered to.

Once the Great Depression hit, cheap hot dogs ceased to be merely novelty street fare and became a budget-friendly necessity for nearly everyone. Vendors responded to the demand by piling dogs high with cheap toppings like potatoes, onions, and other vegetables, many of them pickled (to eliminate the need for pesky expiration dates). The hot dog had gone from snack to meal, but as the effects of the Depression

DOGS AND DIPLOMACY

In June 1939, President Franklin D. Roosevelt hosted a shindig for the king and queen of England at his estate in Hyde Park, New York. The all-American fare of choice? Hot dogs, served on a silver tray but eaten off paper plates. The king had two; the queen, confused about how to consume the colonial construction, was reportedly told by Roosevelt to "push it into your mouth and keep pushing until it is all gone." She used a knife and fork.

Hot dogs met the cold war in 1959 when Nikita Khrushchev stopped in Des Moines, Iowa, on a tour of the U.S. heartland. At a packing plant, the Soviet leader sampled his first sausage-in-a-bun—after his security team skimmed it with a Geiger counter, of course. In 1999, President Bill Clinton brought Israeli Prime Minister Ehud Barak and Palestinian leader Yasser Arafat to the table . . . the picnic table, where kosher hot dogs (and presumably some peace talk) were the order of the day.

waned, it reclaimed its status as fun food. America had caught a glimpse of hot dogs topped by condiments, and regional specialties took off as street vendors, diner cooks, and restaurant chefs looked to create the newest, most crowd-pleasing dog. Meanwhile, the hot dog traveled north to Canada and into the American South. Coleslaw, baked beans, and barbecue all found their way on to the hot dog. Farther south into Mexico and west toward California, fresh vegetables, spicy salsas and sauces, and a whole host of other regional toppings joined the game.

Then, like so many other American eats, the hot dog went global. It traveled back to Europe, to Central and South America, and across the Pacific to Asia and Oceania. The world saw why America had become obsessed with this quick and easy food, and they wanted to put their own spin on it. Hot dogs, frankfurters, and wieners soon shared the spotlight with Polish sausage, bratwurst, *rød pølse*, and *boerewors*. Buns got swapped for flat breads, crispy rolls, baguettes, and batters, and toppings took on a life of their own.

And so the haute dog was born.

THE BASICS

Before we jump into the recipes, there are a few things you need to know about hot dogs. In this section you'll find notes on ingredients, instructions for more than 10 ways to cook a hot dog, tricks for measuring (hint: you don't), and guidelines for assembling a truly superb hot dog (pro tip: you always dress the dog, not the bun).

INGREDIENTS

There are two things you must have to call something a hot dog: a bun and a sausage. But for a *good* hot dog, you need a third component: toppings.

THE BUN

The bun is there to support the sausage and its toppings. Too small and it will fall apart; too big and bread will overpower the dog and the toppings. Feel free to get fancy with your buns, but I'll almost always choose a classic bun, those soft white ones you find in packages of 8 in the grocery store. But don't let that stop you. Pizza bread, Italian loaves, potato rolls, French baguettes, flat bread, and various batters are used all over the globe, and for good reason: they're all delicious. Pay attention to the size and softness of a bun when choosing toppings because a big dog can quickly turn a small bun into an overloaded mess on your plate.

THE SAUSAGE

Here is where hot dogs start to get interesting. There are three key factors in a sausage: meat, casing, and size.

THE MEAT

Nearly all the hot dogs found around the world, and in the recipes in this book, are made with beef, pork, or a mixture of the two. You can also find hot dogs made with chicken, turkey, veal, lamb, bison, and just about any exotic meat you can think of. If meat's not your thing, there's a whole host of dogs made with soy, vegetables, and other healthy (but tasty!) stuff. Mass-produced hot dogs, like those found in grocery stores, will typically contain poultry and various nonmeat fillers like grains and soy as a cheaper alternative to beef and pork alone. For the best flavor, stick to all-meat dogs, preferably those using just beef or pork.

Beef: All-beef hot dogs or sausages are easy to find countrywide. They started as a product of the large kosher communities on the East Coast and today reign supreme as the classic New York dog. Looking for something a little more substantial? Try farmer's sausage, an all-beef smoked sausage you can commonly find in grocery stores.

Pork: Pork is another common hot dog or sausage meat, especially outside the United States. Pork hot dogs, or frankfurters, were inspired by the all-pork sausages of Frankfurt, Germany.

Beef and Pork Mix: A beef and pork mix, or wiener, is the second most common hot dog or sausage. They take their name from the smoked sausages of Johann George Lahner in Vienna (Wien), Austria.

Exotic Meats: Although you won't find any recipes in this book calling for exotic meats, if you can grind it, you can technically make it into a sausage or hot dog: chicken, turkey, alligator—even kangaroo.

Other ingredients: Hot dogs and sausages don't vary only in their meat. Spices, herbs, flavorings, and even the color can change from one variety to another. Though nearly all store-bought hot dogs are artificially dyed to create a more appealing color, certain dogs like the *rød pølse* are heavily dyed to a bright red hue. Garlic is a common ingredient in many hot dogs and sausages and can vary in intensity across brands and regions. Germany's bratwurst is commonly made with spices such as nutmeg and mace and left uncured, whereas other sausages famous to Germany are loaded with spices and smoked.

THE CASING

Casings refer to the material used to create the characteristic tube shape of hot dogs and sausages. Most grocery-store hot dogs are skinless (they're cooked in an artificial or plastic casing that is removed before packaging); most sausages and many hot dogs found at street carts and in restaurants have a natural casing. Natural casings are made from the intestines, specifically the submucosa (a thin layer of connective tissue in the intestines), of various animals, usually the cow, hog, or sheep. When cooked properly, natural casings give the dog a crisp snap, or bite. Artificial casings can also be made using either collagen from animals or cellulose from plants. For sausages, I reccomend hog casings; for hot dogs, I suggest the smaller sheep or lamb casings, which will create a hot dog whose size is similar to those you can find in the grocery store. If you want a super-thick hot dog, there's no reason why you can't use a beef casing instead.

THE SIZE

There are six-inchers, foot-longs, thin hot dogs, thick sausages, split dogs, and everything in between. Hot dog size is a matter of choice and depends on how hungry you are. Just make sure you've got a suitable bun.

THE TOPPINGS

Toppings are what take a dog from ho-hum to haute. Today you can find everything from pickles to fried eggs, shrimp salad to wasabi mayo, and absolutely no ketchup to tons of ketchup on hot dogs.

SAFE COOKING TEMPERATURES

The USDA and FDA recommend the following safe cooking temperatures for meats, especially any that are not precooked.

Fresh Cuts (Beef, Pork and Lamb)	145°F
Ground Meats (Beef, Pork, Lamb, and Poultry)	165°F
Fresh Chicken and Poultry	165°F
Cured Sausage	160°F
Uncured (Fresh) Sausage	160°F to 165°F

To measure temperature, stick a meat thermometer into the thickest part of the cut without touching bone or fat. For homemade sausage or hot dogs, stick the thermometer into the sausage from the bottom, making sure it reaches the center of the link.

There are many ways to cook a hot dog, with each creating a distinctly different eating experience, from the crunchy snap of a fire-charred dog to the mouthwatering bite of a tender, juicy simmered frankfurter. Methods are ordered here from quickest to longest cooking time, starting with the dreaded microwave, which can have you eating a piping-hot hot dog in a minute flat, all the way up to smoking, which can take upwards of three to four hours.

Since most hot dogs and many sausages are precooked, these methods serve to reheat them. Take care when cooking raw hot dogs or sausages to ensure they reach the safe cooking temperature.

Fresh vs. Precooked: The times listed here are for heating pre-cooked hot dogs and sausages. Anytime you are cooking fresh sausage, you must make sure to cook it long enough so that the entire sausage is cooked through or to a temperature of 160°F or 165°F. Unless you're eating *rouchang*, or a cold plain hot dog as it is often eaten in China. If so, just make sure it's below 40°F.

Microwave

RESULT: Quick hot dogs
COOKING TIME: 1 minute
COOKING TEMP: Very high

Microwaves: the hot dog killer. But have no fear. I've found the secret to cooking a decent hot dog in the microwave. Is it as good as grilling, deep-frying, or cooking on a flattop? Nope. Not even close. But it's darn quick and if done right, it can make a great dog in a pinch.

1. Wrap the hot dog tightly in a dry paper towel, curling the ends under the dog so they don't flip open.

2. Place wrapped hot dog on a plate and microwave for 30 to 45 seconds on 80 percent power, or until heated through.

HANDLING: Avoid puncturing hot dogs before, during, or right after cooking; doing so will cause the hot dog to lose a lot of its liquid.

Open Flame

RESULT: Quick, charred hot dogs
COOKING TIME: 2 to 5 minutes
COOKING TEMP: Very high

Open flame cooking is technically similar to grilling (using very hot direct heat), but I've made it its own cooking method because it's a lot more fun, perfect for campfires and cold evenings around a fire pit. It creates a charred, wonderfully crispy skin and a juicy, piping-hot interior. Tongs are the best tool, but you can also use a skewer, though the pierced hot dog will leak fat, juices, and flavor while cooking. It is as simple as cooking a hot dog directly over or, if you're a kid, inside a fire.

1. Prepare a fire.

2. Using long tongs, hold the hot dog a few inches above the tops of the flames. Slowly rotate dog while cooking for about 2 to 5 minutes, or until the skin is charred and crispy and the interior is cooked through.

Grill (or Broil)

RESULT: Charred hot dogs
COOKING TIME: 6 to 8 minutes
COOKING TEMP: High

Grilling and broiling are intense dry-cooking methods that rely on direct heat. But that intensity doesn't mean grilling is too much for an amazing hot dog—in fact, that's what makes the grilled dog so good. Grilling over a flame is the only way to get a char, and both grilling and broiling will create a crispy skin on dogs with natural casings. If you don't have a grill, broiling is essentially the same process except that it uses top-down heat instead of bottom-up heat.

Fun fact: Toasters are essentially little grills for the kitchen—great for buns, not so much for dogs.

1. Preheat a grill to its hottest setting for at least 30 minutes. If using a charcoal grill, heat the charcoal for 30 to 45 minutes, or until the coals ash over. You can also use a chimney starter to get the coals hot. Just before grilling, lower heat to medium (about 400°F). For charcoal, once coals ash over, spread them over the bottom of the grill.

2. Place hot dogs on the grill grates and cook for 3 to 4 minutes, or until charred but not blackened. Flip and cook for another 3 to 4 minutes.

TOASTING BUNS
Place buns cut side down on the grill during the last minute of cooking.

Flattop (or Panfry)

RESULT: Crisp hot dogs
COOKING TIME: 6 to 8 minutes
COOKING TEMP: High

Cooking on flattops is often referred to as grilling because it involves often very high heat diffused through a flat surface. But unlike grilling, flattop cooking produces little smoke, which is why it's popular for front-of-house cooking at restaurants like hibachi grills and Mongolian barbecue joints. It's also one of the most used cooking methods for hot dogs at street carts and in diners. Since flattops aren't common in most homes, you can mimic the results with an electric or stove-top griddle, a large flat cast-iron skillet, or even a large frying pan.

1. Heat the flattop, griddle, or skillet over medium-high heat. Lightly coat the cooking surface with oil, butter, or animal fat. (See the note on page 18 for more on selecting oil.)

2. Place the hot dog on the flattop and cook for 3 to 4 minutes, or until browned and crispy. Flip and cook for another 3 to 4 minutes, until second side has browned and crisped as well.

Flattop cookware was first used centuries ago to cook corn dough in Mexico and Central America. The Spanish adopted the method and called it cooking *a la plancha*, meaning "grilled on a plate."

Panfry toppings just before cooking hot dogs so that you'll be ready to serve them hot off the grill. Added bonus: Panfrying on the same flattop as was used for the toppings gives hot dogs a richer flavor.

MORE WAYS TO PANFRY

Use this versatile cooking method for split dogs (page 43), toasted buns, and crispy pan-fried toppings.

FLATTOP METHOD FOR SPLIT DOGS: The Split Dog is achieved by butterflying the hot dog, or slicing it almost in half lengthwise, and frying it on a flattop as described above.

FLATTOP METHOD FOR TOASTED BUNS: Place bun on a dry portion of the flattop for the last 30 seconds to 1 minute of cooking.

FLATTOP METHOD TO SWEAT TOPPINGS: Heat a little butter or oil on a flattop over low heat. Cook the ingredients, stirring or tossing occasionally, until they are soft but not brown.

FLATTOP METHOD FOR SAUTÉED TOPPINGS: Heat a little butter or oil in a skillet or on a flattop over medium-high heat. Cook the ingredients, stirring or tossing frequently, until they begin to brown and soften. Cook for a few minutes more if you want crispy toppings.

Deep-Fry

USES: Juicy, greasy hot dogs, split dogs, corn dogs, and other battered dogs
COOKING TIME: 4 to 6 minutes
COOKING TEMP: Medium-high

As with practically every food out there, hot dogs taste great when they are deep-fried. Deep-fat frying is a great way to cook bacon-wrapped dogs to a perfect crisp. It's also used for corn dogs and other batter-dipped dogs.

1. Heat oil in a fryer or large pot with tall sides to 350°F. (Oil should be about 6 inches deep.) Spread newspaper or paper towels over your counter and put a metal rack on top. Have oven mitts and a kitchen thermometer at the ready.

2. *For wieners:* Place hot dogs in oil, a few at a time so you don't crowd them, and cook for 4 to 6 minutes, or until they begin to brown and are cooked through. *For battered dogs:* Place battered dogs in hot oil a few at a time so that the batter doesn't touch (the dogs will fuse). Try to keep sticks out of the oil, for ease of handling. Cook for about 5 minutes, or until batter begins to turn a golden light brown.

3. Remove dogs from oil using metal tongs or a slotted spoon and let drip-dry on the metal rack.

Deep-fry to the Max: To create a deep fried-dog that's bursting at the seams, leave the dog in the fryer a little longer, until it splits open.

TYPES OF OILS

Available today are a wide variety of oils, from the standard soybean oil (often sold as vegetable oil), canola oil, olive oil, and peanut oil all the way on to corn, grapeseed, olive, safflower, and sunflower oil. But which is best for deep-frying? Most important, you need an oil with a high smoking point (e.g., canola, corn, safflower, sunflower, soybean, or vegetable oil). You will also want to consider the oil's flavor. Most oils, aside from olive, sesame, and peanut, are bland and will have almost no effect on the flavor of the item being fried. Peanut oil is wonderful for frying because of the nutty flavor it can impart. I typically use soybean oil for most items, and sometimes peanut oil for fries.

Deep-fat fryers are increasingly popular in home kitchens, but you can deep-fry dogs without investing in serious equipment. Just use a Dutch oven or any large, tall, heavy-bottomed pot; the sides will help protect against splatters, and the thick bottom will keep the oil at an even temperature. No matter what equipment you use, hot oil can splatter and bubble up unexpectedly. Always use caution and common sense.

Simmer or Boil

RESULT: Moist hot dogs
COOKING TIME: 8 to 10 minutes
COOKING TEMP: Low

Like steaming, simmering and boiling are moist cooking methods; however, both require cooking hot dogs submerged in water and at varying degrees of heat and intensity. Water boils at 212°F and creates rapid large bubbles. Simmering occurs at lower temperatures (around 180–195°F) and creates smaller, less frequent bubbles. I suggest simmering instead of boiling, because it's a gentler cooking process with less risk of overcooking or splitting the dogs.

1. In a saucepan over medium-high heat, bring enough water to cover the dogs to a simmer.

2. Place hot dogs in the simmering water and cook for 8 to 10 minutes, or until they reach an internal temperature of 160°F.

> *"Put a pint of Claret to a quart of Water, put in some sweet herbs finely shred, a blade or two of Mace, and some Cinamon, let them boyl about a quarter of an hour, then serve them up with beaten Ginger, Cinamon or Mustard and Sugar, in Sawcers."*
>
> —17th-century recipe for "Sausages to Boyl"

> Dirty Water Bath: You can leave hot dogs in simmering water (or warm water, so long as it is above 160°F) to keep them warm.

FLAVORFUL DIRTY WATER BATH: Add seasonings like garlic, onion, and herbs to flavor the hot dog while cooking. You can also replace the water with broth, beer, or other liquids to add more flavor to the dog.

ECUADORIAN WATER BATH: Add 5 halved garlic cloves, a handful chopped tomatoes and chopped onion, and a spoonful of your favorite hot sauce to the water before adding the hot dogs.

Roast

RESULT: Worry-free bulk hot dogs
COOKING TIME: 10 to 20 minutes
COOKING TEMP: Medium

Roasting is a fairly easy way to cook a bunch of hot dogs at once: there's a lot more space on a baking sheet than there is in a frying pan, after all. Simply set them in the oven and cook until heated through.

Preheat oven to 350°F. Place the hot dogs on a baking sheet lined with parchment paper. Roast for 10 to 20 minutes, or until hot dogs are heated through to 160°F.

ROASTING IN ADVANCE

Set the oven to Warm or 160°F and leave the hot dogs in the oven for up to 1 hour to keep them hot. Keep an eye on them: compared to a dirty water bath or a hot dog roller, this method will dry out the dogs quicker.

Roller

RESULT: Warm hot dogs for extended periods
COOKING TIME: 8 to 10 minutes
COOKING TEMP: Low

Chances are you've seen shriveled-up hot dogs rolling away on one of these machines in a corner store or gas station shop. And you probably don't have a hot dog roller at home . . . so this method might not seem worth it. However, just like dirty water dogs, roller dogs are scrumptious in their own right, and this is a great way to keep hot dogs hot for up to 4 hours. This method is best for heating precooked dogs, not for cooking raw dogs. Is it worth running out and buying an industrial hot dog roller? Nah. Did I let that stop me? Nope. I love my hot dog roller. Take it from me: the odd stares from your friends will disappear when they taste their first roller dog.

1. Turn on the machine to medium-high.

2. Place hot dogs on the rollers and cook for 8 to 10 minutes, or until hot.

3. Turn the machine to low/medium-low (make sure it is set to keep the dogs at 160°F) to keep the hot dogs warm for up to 4 hours.

> You can find hot dog rollers at specialty stores as well as on eBay and Amazon. Look for one that lets you control the temperature of the rollers and has enough room for at least 8 dogs. (See Sources, page 162.)

Steam

RESULT: Moist hot dogs
COOKING TIME: 10 to 12 minutes
COOKING TEMP: Low

Steaming is a moist cooking method, meaning it relies on water. It is the gentlest cooking method and yields a tender and (surprise!) moist hot dog. This is also one of the best ways to warm a bun, too. But be careful—steaming a hot dog with a casing for too long may cause it to split, which can release the dog's fat and juices (i.e., flavor).

1. Pour an inch of water into a pot large enough to hold a steam tray or vegetable steamer. Bring water to a boil over high heat, then reduce heat to low to maintain a simmer.

2. Place tray or steamer in the pot and arrange the hot dogs so they don't touch the water. Cover the pot and cook for 10 to 12 minutes, or until the hot dogs are cooked to an internal temperature of 160°F. (So long as the water does not reach the hot dogs, you can use any device with holes, including sieves and colanders, assuming they will fit in the pot.) To steam the buns, place them alongside the dogs on the tray or steamer during the last minute of cooking.

Barbecue (or Smoke)

RESULT: Smoky flavor and rich color
(when cooking raw hot dogs and sausages)
COOKING TIME: 1 to 4 hours
COOKING TEMP: Very low

Smoking is a slow cooking process that requires a very low temperature and, well, smoke. To smoke hot dogs and sausages, the raw, often cured, links are hung in smokehouses (large rooms for commercial hot dog makers, and small spaces for you and me), then subjected to low, usually indirect heat and the smoke from various types of wood, depending on the desired flavor. Smoking is a vital step in the manufacture of almost all hot dogs, because it, along with nitrates, is what gives the wiener its distinctive red color and lightly smoky flavor. Typically hot dogs are only partially smoked (then boiled after smoking); by contrast, sausages are often smoked completely, requiring no additional cooking. The long cooking time gives the hot dog or sausage a chance to absorb the flavors from the smoke. and the low temperature keeps the fat from rendering. When smoking, you'll want to use curing agents in the sausage and be sure that their internal temperature reaches 160°F before removing them from the smoker.

1. Soak wood chips in water for 1 hour before smoking.

2. Set up the smoker and heat it to 170°F.

3. Smoke the hot dog or sausages in the smoker until the internal temperature reaches 160°F, about 3 to 4 hours. (For hot dogs that you will smoke only partially, smoke for 1 to 2 hours and then finish the cooking using the simmering method, again being sure that the dog's internal temperature reaches 160°F.) Replace wood chips every 60 to 90 minutes to ensure adequate smoking. For a less smoky flavor, stop adding wood chips after the first hour.

4. Place hot dogs or sausages in a large bowl filled with ice water and let sit for 10 minutes to stop the cooking.

5. Hang hot dogs or sausages on racks or hooks in your kitchen, or in a cool dry place at room temperature, to dry for 2 hours. (Do not leave the sausages at room temperature any longer because they will spoil.) Serve or refrigerate.

TYPE OF SMOKE

Depending on the type of wood used for smoking, you can achieve wildly varying tastes, from the heavy flavor of hickory to the subtler flavor of oak, alder, or apple. I like hickory for smoking sausage, though many people find it too strong. You can buy food-grade wood chips at just about any market or store that sells BBQ and grilling equipment. For wood chip sources, see page 162.

MEASURING

If there's one rule to follow with hot dogs, it's that you should never measure the toppings. I have, however, included some handy guidelines for how much of an ingredient a hot dog tends to use, just in case you're trying a frankfurter from a country halfway around the world, or you forget how much mustard or onions you like.

A DROP: A drop is technically defined as $1/96$th of a teaspoon. Here, we'll call it one drop from a hot sauce bottle.

A PINCH: Officially $1/16$ of a teaspoon, a pinch here is the amount of something you can pinch between two fingers.

A DASH: $1/8$ teaspoon—call it a couple pinches.

A SPRINKLING: A little more than a dash, and enough to cover something lightly.

A SQUIRT OR A LINE: That perfect amount that comes from gently squeezing a bottled condiment as you draw it over a dog.

A SMEAR: A bit more than a line, and enough just to cover the top of a dog.

TO COAT: Whether on a dog or a bun, this is enough to cover the whole surface.

A SPOONFUL: Take an average spoon from your kitchen drawer and fill it up.

A PALMFUL: Pour the contents into a cupped hand until your palm is covered.

A HANDFUL: Pour the contents into a cupped hand until your palm and fingers are hidden.

A PILE: An overflowing handful.

A HEAPING PILE: Enough to fill two handfuls.

AS MUCH AS THE DOG CAN HOLD: This is my favorite. Pile those ingredients on until they start falling off the side of the dog—then add a little more.

EIGHTY-SIX: Omit this ingredient normally used from the dog or recipe.

DOUBLE: Measure out twice as much as normal.

TRIPLE: Measure out three times as much as normal.

HALVE: Measure out half as much as normal.

WHY ARE OUNCES LISTED?

Measuring by weight when baking is a far more precise means of ensuring consistency than measuring by volume. Don't worry: there is nothing wrong with using trusty measuring cups and spoons. When measuring an ingredient like flour by volume, first fluff up the flour with a spoon to make it light and airy. Then gently draw the measuring cup through the flour and swipe the straight edge of a knife across the top of the cup to level the flour. Be sure not to pack the flour in the measuring cup.

ASSEMBLY

Now that we've discussed how to prep and portion ingredients, it's time to talk about assembly. Poorly constructed hot dogs are a major disappointment, but they are so easy to prevent. Just use these steps as your guide.

STEP ONE: PREPARE YOUR INGREDIENTS. Ready all your toppings ahead of time so they don't slow down the assembly. That includes making more involved toppings, like fries or chilis, as well as any homemade condiments you would like to use.

STEP TWO: GET OUT YOUR BUNS. Nothing will show guests you're an amateur hot dog maker more than forgetting to get out your buns or, worse, forgetting to buy enough of them. (Be warned: Packs of hot dogs and packages of buns do not always contain equal numbers.) For a truly special meal, bake your own hot dog buns from scratch using one of the recipes on pages 129–132.

STEP THREE: COOK THE HOT DOGS. Unless you've got a water bath or a hot dog roller ready, only cook as many dogs as you need right away. You are not allowed, under any circumstance, to make haute dogs ahead of time. They must be made to order so they're piping hot and fresh.

STEP FOUR: TOAST OR WARM THE BUNS. Have them at the ready (see Step Two) and make sure to toast, warm, or steam them toward the end of cooking the hot dog so they'll be warm when you serve them. Don't heat them after the dogs are done or the hot dogs will get cold—it's all about timing.

STEP FIVE: PUT THE DOG IN THE BUN. The wiener goes in first, before any condiments.

STEP SIX: DRESS THE DOG. Condiments and toppings are meant to enhance the flavor of the dog, so spread them, pile them, and sprinkle them on the frankfurter—not the bun. Make sure to follow the special order of toppings (though some hot dogs break this rule, so pay attention to each recipe's instructions): Condiments like mustard, mayo, or ketchup first. Chilies, sauces, and big-ticket items like coleslaw, baked beans, or shrimp salad next. Fresh vegetables and spices last. Voilà!

STEP SEVEN: SERVE. Get those hot haute dogs out to everybody, STAT! As the name suggests, hot dogs must be served hot. Oh, and these haute dogs are never too big to eat with your hands, so go whole hog and give it a try.

STEP EIGHT: REPEAT. Start from the beginning and make yourself another haute dog. You know you want one.

THE HAUTE DOGS

AMERICAN
CLASSICS

THE PLAIN JANE • Inside-Out Dog

THE NEW YORK STYLE HOT DOG • THE DEPRESSION DOG

THE CHICAGO DOG • The Rule-Breaker • CONEY ISLAND DOG

Flint-Style Coney Dog • TEXAS HOT DOG • MICHIGAN DOG

NEW YORK SYSTEM WIENER • WHITE HOT • RED HOT • RED SNAPPER

ITALIAN DOG • MONTREAL STEAMIE • HALF-SMOKE • D.C. Street Cart Style

SLAW DOG • CORN DOG • Funnel Cake Dog • Beer Batter Dog

Corn Brat • WAFFLE DOG • Maple Syrup Breakfast Dog

Spicy Waffle Dog

THE PLAIN JANE

THE PLAIN JANE IS THE PERFECT ILLUSTRATION OF HOW EACH COOKING method influences the flavor and experience of a dog. The ingredients are simple, but by grilling the hot dog and toasting the bun, you get a deliciously charred, smoky flavor and a hot dog perfect for any backyard gathering. Serve it plain or add classic toppings.

Classic bun
Beef and pork hot dog
Spicy yellow mustard

Kitchen Note: See From-Scratch Ingredients (page 127) for recipes for classic buns, beef and pork hot dogs, and spicy yellow mustard.

ASSEMBLY: Split open a classic bun. Grill the beef and pork hot dog, and toast the bun on the grill just before serving (see page 16 for instructions). Place the dog in the bun and smear a generous portion of spicy yellow mustard on the dog.

Mustard takes its name from the Latin word *mustum*, meaning "new wine." The condiment was first made by combining wine must with the ground seeds of the mustard plant.

INSIDE-OUT DOG: Split the cooked hot dog like you would a bun: cut into it lengthwise enough to open it, but not enough to slice it into two pieces. Place half of a classic bun in the dog and top with a smear of mustard.

THE NEW YORK STYLE HOT DOG

Place of Origin: NEW YORK CITY ★ Other Names: DIRTY WATER DOG, NEW YORK DOG

FEW CITIES ARE AS SYNONYMOUS WITH THE HOT DOG AS NEW YORK CITY. The history of the hot dog in New York was, for a time at least, the history of the hot dog itself. Heck, it is rumored that the word "hot dog" was coined at a Giants game—the *New York Journal*'s Tad Dorgan, a cartoonist, needed a cute and memorable name for the handheld treat that the crowd seemed to eat up (in reality, the term was used long before it was ever seen in a Dorgan cartoon). At a time when "hot frankfurters" and "red hots" were common terminology, the hot dog quickly became a street cart favorite, with the large Jewish immigration to New York in the late 19th century fueling the love for the characteristic all-beef dog.

New York Style Sautéed Onions (page 156)
Classic bun
All-beef hot dog
Spicy brown mustard
Sauerkraut

Kitchen Notes: Thick with tomato paste and spices, New York Style Sautéed Onions are something special. Sabrett sells their Sautéed Onion Sauce online if you're craving the real deal (see Sources, page 162). Spicy brown mustard pairs well with all-beef dogs. See page 138 to make your own.

PREP: Make sautéed onions according to the recipe.

ASSEMBLY: Split open a classic bun. Panfry an all-beef hot dog on a flattop; during the last minute of cooking, lightly toast the bun (see page 17). Place the dog in the bun. Add a slathering of spicy brown mustard to the dog. Top with a handful each of sauerkraut and sautéed onions.

New York City street cart dogs are famous for being juicy and having the characteristic bite of a natural casing. For a similar result, buy all-beef hot dogs that say "natural casing" on the package. Some of New York's most popular brands are Sabrett and Nathan's Famous.

DIRTY WATER WHAT?

Dirty water dogs are so named because they are stored in hot water bins in streetside food carts—throughout the day, small amounts of juices and fat slowly leak from the dog, making the water cloudy. (For more on making your own dirty water dogs, see page 19.)

THE DEPRESSION DOG

THE DEPRESSION DOG, OR THE ORIGINAL CHICAGO DOG, IS THE FIRST "dragged-through-the-garden" dog, a term reflecting the copious amounts of vegetables and toppings found on this Midwestern wiener. In fact, you'd barely notice the original Chicago Dog next to its modern namesake (see page 32). Looking for a way to cheaply feed patrons during the Great Depression, street vendors added whatever they could find to the dog and bun, an array that typically included mustard, onions, sport peppers, sometimes relish, and a huge pile of potatoes. Today, classic Depression Dogs are served with fries instead of potatoes.

Thick-cut fries (page 154)
Poppy seed or classic bun
All-beef hot dog
Yellow mustard
Diced white onions
Whole sport peppers
Classic relish

Kitchen Notes: Sport peppers are small pickled peppers popular in Chicago and the American South, among other regions. They can be green, yellow, red, or a mix of colors; though mild ones are available, burning-hot varieties are most common. If you can't get them locally, see Sources (page 162) to order a jar, or substitute pepperoncini or tabasco peppers. See the recipes listed on page 127 for from-scratch ingredients, from fries and poppy seed buns to hot dogs and condiments.

PREP: Make fries according to the recipe and set aside.

ASSEMBLY: Get out a poppy seed bun. Cook an all-beef hot dog by simmering or panfrying it on a flattop (page 19). Place the hot dog in the bun and top with a single line of yellow mustard, a handful of diced onions, a few sport peppers, and a spoonful or two of classic relish. Top with as many fries as the dog will hold, or serve them on the side.

HOT DOGS IN HISTORY: DOGS AS CONTRABAND MULES

Not everyone loved hot dogs in the early 20th century. Many saw them as symbolic of the seedy underbelly of simmering American corruption, and in 1921 the *Los Angeles Times* ran the screaming headline *Secret of Hot Dog is Exposed*. The secret in question? "Innocent-Looking Sandwich Found to Contain Moonshine," the result of the brilliant (though questionable) smuggling methods of one enterprising bootlegger.

THE CHICAGO DOG

Place of Origin: CHICAGO, IL ★ Other Names: CHAR DOG, CHICAGO RED HOT

THE PICKLES, TOMATOES, CELERY SALT, NEON-GREEN RELISH, AND OTHER vegetables common to the modern Chicago Dog were introduced a few decades after the Depression (and the original Depression Dog). So how did this modern vegetable-laden version come to be? Some claim it was the work of Vienna Beef and its marketing department (some Depression Dog purists even go as far as to claim that Vienna Beef added pickles to the Chicago Dog to drive up pickle sales after the company purchased a pickle factory). Whether you believe Vienna Beef had a hand in its genesis, one thing is certain: you must keep the ketchup bottle far, far away. In fact, it's against Illinois state law to add ketchup to the Chicago Dog. (Okay, I made that part up. But seriously—no ketchup on these dogs.)

Poppy seed or classic bun
All-beef hot dog
Yellow mustard
Neon-green relish
Tomato wedges
Whole sport peppers
Dill pickle spear
Celery salt

Kitchen Notes: The idea of making neon-green relish at home might seem farfetched. But it's easy to do, and the result is tasty, brightly hued (thanks to a few drops of food coloring), and preservative free (see recipe, page 161). For more on sport peppers and where to find them, see the note on page 31.

ASSEMBLY: Get out a poppy seed bun and a setup to steam it. Panfry an all-beef hot dog on a flattop; toward the end of cooking, steam the bun (see page 20 for instructions). Place the dog in the bun. Top with a line of yellow mustard, a spoonful or two of neon-green relish, tomato wedges, sport peppers, and a dill pickle spear. Sprinkle with a dash of celery salt. And don't even think about adding ketchup.

"Nobody, I mean nobody, puts ketchup on a hot dog." —Harry Callahan (Clint Eastwood) in *Sudden Impact*

THE RULE-BREAKER: Add a couple spoonfuls of tomato sauce and a big squirt of ketchup on top.

CONEY ISLAND DOG

Place of Origin: DETROIT, MI ★ Other Names: CONEY DOG, DETROIT DOG

THE CHILI TOPPING ON THIS LOADED DOG WAS THE BRILLIANT IDEA OF THE Greek and Macedonian chefs of the Midwest. And, as for the New York Style Dog and various Chicago Dogs, countless versions exist—each restaurant puts its own spin on the spices, sauce, and toppings. The purist will take his Coney Island Dog only with a runny, beanless chili (aka Coney sauce), diced onions, and yellow mustard. Despite its moniker, the Coney Island Dog comes from Michigan. The name is merely an homage to the birthplace of the hot dog and the many immigrants who stopped in New York on their way to Detroit in the early 20th century. Confusingly enough, in Coney Island this chili-topped special is known as a Michigander or Michigan Dog, which shouldn't be confused with *another* variety of chili dog that goes by the same name in other parts of the States (see page 39).

Coney Island Sauce (store-bought or from scratch, page 153)
Classic bun
All-beef hot dog
Yellow mustard
Diced white onions

Kitchen Note: Many grocery stores stock canned Coney sauce alongside other chilis and sauces.

PREP: Make sauce according to the recipe, or heat store-bought chili sauce until hot.

ASSEMBLY: Get out a classic bun. Panfry an all-beef hot dog on a flattop, as on page 17. Place the dog in the bun. Top with a smear of mustard, a heaping pile of Coney sauce, and a handful of diced onions.

FLINT-STYLE CONEY DOG: Use a drier ground beef chili (store-bought or from scratch, page 153) instead of Coney sauce and, if possible, a Koegel Coney hot dog. (Koegel is the favored brand in and around Flint, Michigan; for where to buy their dogs, see Sources, page 162.)

TEXAS HOT DOG

Place of Origin: NEW JERSEY OR PENNSYLVANIA ★ Other Names: TEXAS HOT

LIKE CONEY ISLAND DOGS, TEXAS HOT DOGS WERE FIRST MADE IN A LAND far from the place for which they're named. Texas Dogs hail from either Pennsylvania or New Jersey, depending on which hot dog fanatic you ask. And, in another similarity to Coney Island Dogs, their name is an homage to a state that is famous for its chili eaters. But instead of being cooked on a flattop like a Coney Dog, this wiener is deep-fried. The sauce is typically more akin to *saltsa kima* (Greek meat sauce) than a true Texas chili, and it's less runny than the one that tops its cousin from Michigan. This frankfurter always gets spicy mustard instead of yellow, which adds even more kick.

Greek Sauce (page 153)
Classic bun
Beef and pork hot dog
Spicy yellow mustard
Diced white onions

Kitchen Notes: To try recipes for homemade buns, beef and pork hot dogs, and spicy yellow mustard, see page 127. Popular store-bought varieties of spicy yellow mustard include French's, Gulden's, Inglehoffer, and Woeber's Sweet Hot Mister Mustard.

PREP: Make Greek sauce according to the recipe.

ASSEMBLY: Get out a classic bun and a setup to steam it. Deep-fry a beef and pork hot dog and steam the bun (as on pages 18 and 20). Place the dog in the bun. Top with a slathering of spicy yellow mustard, a heaping pile of Greek sauce, and a handful of diced onions.

Secret's in the Sauce: Greek Sauce is similar to chili and easy to make; see how on page 153. In the northeastern United States and other parts of the world, you may be able to find prepared Greek meat sauce (*saltsa kima*) in the canned chili section of the grocery store or at international and specialty food stores; see Sources, page 162.

MICHIGAN DOG

Place of Origin: MICHIGAN ★ Other Names: THE MICHIGAN, THE MICHIGANER

YOU MAY THINK I'M JUST SPLITTING HAIRS NOW. WHAT CAN POSSIBLY MAKE this chili dog different from the previous two? Well, for one thing, this dog *does* come from Michigan, although you wouldn't call it a "Michigan Dog" in Michigan—that would be too easy. This hot dog is popular all over the northeast United States and across the border in Quebec, and its many iterations all use a tomato-based sauce, like the recipe here. If you're looking for a spicy, tomato-heavy take on the chili dog, the Michigan Dog is the wiener for you.

Tomato-Based Chili Sauce (store-bought or from scratch, page 153)
Classic bun
All-beef hot dog
Yellow mustard
Diced white onions
Hot sauce, optional

PREP: Prepare the tomato-based chili sauce according to the recipe, or heat store-bought tomato-based chili sauce until hot. (If you can't find a tomato chili, simply add a 16-ounce can of stewed tomatoes and their juices to store-bought chili before heating.)

ASSEMBLY: Get out a classic bun. Panfry an all-beef hot dog on a flattop (as on page 17). Place the dog in the bun. Top with a huge pile of chili, a handful of diced onions, and a thin line of yellow mustard. Add a few drops of hot sauce on top, if desired.

NEW YORK SYSTEM WIENER

Place of Origin: RHODE ISLAND ★ Other Names: HOT WIENER, CONEY ISLAND SYSTEM DOG

THIS DOG IS YET ANOTHER THAT HAS NO GRASP OF AMERICAN GEOGRAPHY. The New York System Wiener comes from Rhode Island but is named after the veritable home of the American hot dog, Coney Island, and a dog that it no longer resembles. The name was a marketing ploy created to bank on the popularity of food and culture in and around New York City.

Rhode Island Chili, aka Rhode Island meat sauce (page 153)
Classic bun
Pork and veal hot dog
Yellow mustard
Diced white onions
Celery salt

Kitchen Notes: The secret to a good Rhode Island chili is using ground beef that is no more than 80 percent lean. This spicy chili can be made in advance—it keeps for up to 1 week in an airtight container in the refrigerator, or up to 1 month in the freezer. Pork and veal hot dogs can be found at many grocery stores and butchers (see Sources, page 162); they're also delicious when homemade. Flip to page 127 for hot dog, bun, and condiment recipes.

PREP: Make Rhode Island chili according to the recipe and warm it on the stove or in the microwave until hot.

ASSEMBLY: Get out a classic bun and a setup to steam it. Panfry a pork and veal hot dog using the flattop method and steam the bun (pages 17 and 20). Place the dog in the bun. Top with a line of yellow mustard, a large helping of meat sauce, a handful of diced onions, and a sprinkling of celery salt.

Pork and veal are traditionally used in this dog. The combination of meats has a distinctly delicate flavor that pairs nicely with the spices found in these special dogs.

HOT DOG HISTORY: WIENERS ON WHEELS

The first "wienermobile" was really more of a wagon, driven with a live band of German musicians to advertise the fine sausage products of Oscar F. Mayer in the 1920s. The vehicle took on its trademark tubular shape in 1936, and a whole fleet appeared after World War II. Today, the Oscar Mayer company sees over 1,000 applications annually to become a "hotdogger" behind the weenie wheel of one of their six spiffed-up sausage cars.

WHITE HOT

UPSTATE NEW YORKERS KNOW ABOUT THE WAR OF THE HOTS BETWEEN Rochester and Buffalo: one city takes their hots red, the other white, and there is no compromise between the two. The "white" wieners of the White Hots are made with uncured pork and veal, a derivative of the "white and porkys" enjoyed by the large German community that immigrated to upstate New York in the late 19th and early 20th centuries. Like the original Chicago Dog, these hots came out of Depression-era thrift: butchers and hot dog vendors began putting whatever leftover pieces of meat they could find into the sausages, skipping the curing process altogether for a cheaper, budget-friendly dog. Today the White Hot is just as gourmet as its red counterpart, so have no fear: this is a true *haute* dog.

**Rochester Meat Sauce
  (page 153)**
Classic bun
**Uncured pork and veal
  hot dog**
Spicy brown mustard
Diced white onions

Kitchen Notes: Some Rochester establishments closely guard their meat sauce recipes. Visit the city to taste them all, from Nick Tahou's to Steve T's. Some locations sell their meat sauce in jars to take home. For uncured pork and veal dogs, visit your local butcher or turn to Sources, page 162.

PREP: Make Rochester meat sauce according to the recipe and keep warm.

ASSEMBLY: Get out a classic bun. Panfry an uncured pork and veal dog using the flattop method for split dogs (page 17). Place in the bun and spread a smear of spicy brown mustard over the dog. Top with a heaping pile of Rochester meat sauce and a handful of diced onions.

Nick Tahou's trademarked the original Garbage Plate, but this Rochester delicacy goes by many names: Dinner Plate, Sloppy Plate, Junkyard Plate, even Plat du Refuse, and (vegan) Compost Plate.

SERVE IT AS A PLATE: Assemble a mountainous heap of hot french fries or home fries, cheeseburger or hamburger, white hots and/or red hots—at least two hots per plate, potato salad, macaroni salad, baked beans, and a generous ladleful of meat sauce. Corn bread or a roll on the side is optional, but it makes a handy way to sop up all that sauce.

RED HOT

THE HOT DOG OF CHOICE 80 MILES WEST OF ROCHESTER, IN BUFFALO, THE Red Hot is more traditional than the White Hot. And back in the 1920s, it was the more expensive, gourmet choice. But don't tell a Buffalonian that. Despite the similar names and proximity of their places of origin, these two hots could not be more different. Instead of the uncured and unsmoked wiener that defines the White, the Red features a more traditional red (all-beef) hot dog. Horseradish mustard and chili relish give this dog a spicier bite.

Horseradish Mustard (store-bought or from scratch, page 151)
Chili Relish (store-bought or from scratch, page 161)
Classic bun
All-beef hot dog
Finely chopped white onions

Kitchen Notes: Homemade horseradish mustard packs a punch. Chili relish can be as hot or as mild as you like, depending on the ratio of bell peppers to jalapeño, poblano, and serrano peppers. See recipes on pages 151 and 161.

PREP: Make condiments in advance, if using homemade.

ASSEMBLY: Get out a classic bun. Grill an all-beef hot dog as instructed on page 16. Place the dog in the bun and top with a smear of horseradish mustard, a spoonful or two of chili relish, and a handful of finely chopped onions.

RED SNAPPER

IT IS HARD NOT TO NOTICE THE UNNATURALLY HUED WIENER THAT GIVES the Red Snapper its name. These artificially dyed dogs have been eaten in Maine for decades, and no one's quite sure how they were created. Theories range from a marketing scheme to an overzealous butcher trying to add a little color to an otherwise gray dog. Many hot dogs, especially in the early years when subpar ingredients were the norm, were dyed to appear more natural. Today, hot dog manufacturers still dye their dogs, though few are tinged to the deep color of the wieners used here.

New England–style bun
Red-dyed beef and pork
** hot dog**
Yellow mustard

Kitchen Notes: For where to buy neon-red beef and pork hot dogs, talk to your local butcher or flip to the many online purveyors listed under Sources, page 162. If you find natural-casing red-dyed beef and pork dogs—a Maine delicacy—you can grill or boil them and savor the signature snap with each bite.

ASSEMBLY: Get out a New England–style bun. Grill a red-dyed beef and pork hot dog as instructed on page 16. Place the dog in the bun and top with a smear of yellow mustard.

No Ordinary Bun: New England–style rolls are also known as frankfurter rolls, lobster rolls, and top-loading rolls or buns. They are split on the top instead of on the side, like classic hot dog buns (also known as American-style buns).

ITALIAN DOG

Place of Origin: NEWARK, NJ ★ Other Names: NEW JERSEY POTATO DOG

THOUGH IT MAY SEEM LIKE A MODERN INNOVATION (OR THE CREATION OF A drunk college student), the New Jersey Italian hot dog can be traced back to the 1930s and a little mom-and-pop diner, where the owners served a recipe that had been passed down from an Italian grandmother. Another account traces this dog's story all the way to Italy, where it was common to combine peppers, potatoes, and sausage and serve the mixture in a pocket of bread. No matter the origin, the Italian Dog is a hearty, filling dog packed with flavor.

**Fried Potato Wedges
(page 154)**
Olive oil, for sautéing
Sliced onions
Sliced bell peppers
Pizza bread or Italian roll
2 all-beef hot dogs
Ketchup, optional

Kitchen Notes: Pizza bread is a big, thick, oval loaf that is seriously substantial. The crusty exterior and fluffy interior of a pizza bread or a good Italian roll is essential here, and not just because it's Italian! It must be sturdy enough to support loads of toppings and soft enough to soak up the flavorful drippings. For homemade ketchup recipes, see page 148.

PREP: Make potatoes according to the recipe and keep warm. Next, warm a splash of olive oil in a skillet over medium heat, add onions and peppers, and cook, stirring, for about 8 to 10 minutes, or until soft and translucent.

ASSEMBLY: Get out a loaf of pizza bread or an Italian roll. Deep-fry 2 hot dogs as instructed on page 18. While the dogs cook, use a sharp knife to cut a slit down the center of the bread to create a pocket; do not cut all the way through. Place the wieners in the bread and add a line of ketchup, if desired. Top with a pile of potatoes, onions, and peppers.

QUOMODO "HOT DOG" DICITUR IN LATINE?

In 2003, the Vatican published an updated lexicon of Latin words for all those pesky things invented since the fall of the Roman Empire. Their neologism for hot dog? *Pastillum botello fartum*, literally translated as "a little loaf stuffed with a small sausage."

MONTREAL STEAMIE

THIS DOG CAN BE TRACED BACK TO 1930s MONTREAL, AS THE POPULARITY OF the hot dog in America spread across the border. Despite the city's ban on street carts in the 1940s, the Montreal Steamie has lived on as a classic. Order one "all dressed"—an Anglicization of *tout garni,* which means "all garnished" (i.e., with everything)—and you'll likely get a dog topped with mustard, chopped onions, and 'kraut.

Classic bun
All-beef hot dog
Yellow mustard
Chopped white onions
Sauerkraut

Kitchen Note: "All dressed" doesn't mean you can add ketchup or relish. Skip those condiments for an authentic Montreal Steamie.

ASSEMBLY: Get out a classic bun. Steam an all-beef hot dog and the bun as instructed on page 20. Place the hot dog in the bun and top with a smear of mustard and a handful each of chopped onions and sauerkraut.

HALF-SMOKE

Place of Origin: WASHINGTON, D.C. ★ Other Names: CAPITAL DOG

WHERE THIS DOG DIFFERS FROM MOST IS IN THE USE OF A PORK AND BEEF sausage rather than a frankfurter, making it a handful *and* a mouthful. It's smoked and charred, then topped with a regionally specific meat sauce, like many of the chili dogs of the northeastern United States, and finished with a generous helping of mustard and onions.

District Chili (page 153)
Classic bun
Smoked beef and
   pork sausage
Yellow mustard
Diced white onions

Kitchen Notes: If you really want to go whole hog, make your own classic hot dog buns and yellow mustard; see From-Scratch Ingredients, page 127.

PREP: Prepare chili according to the recipe and keep warm.

ASSEMBLY: Get out a classic bun. Panfry a smoked beef and pork sausage on a flattop (page 17) until charred. Place the sausage in the bun. Add a smear of yellow mustard, a heaping pile of chili, and a handful of diced onions.

D.C. STREET CART STYLE: Add relish and New York Style Sautéed Onions (page 156).

SLAW DOG

Place of Origin: WEST VIRGINIA ★ Other Names: WEST VIRGINIA DOG

COLESLAW (FROM THE DUTCH *KOOLSLA*) HAS BEEN AROUND FOR YEARS, but, like the hot dog, it got a stateside makeover and quickly became an American favorite, especially in the South. Variations of coleslaw-topped dogs dot the region, but many trace their roots back to the hills of West Virginia. Legend has it that south- and westbound travelers picked up a taste for Slaw Dogs in the Mountain State and took them along as they migrated to other areas. In all but the northernmost part of the state, requesting one "with everything" will get you a toasted or steamed bun packed with a juicy grilled hot dog topped with yellow mustard, thick and spicy chili (or "sauce," depending on whom you ask), and a pile of creamy coleslaw.

Classic Hot Dog Chili (store-bought or from scratch, page 153)
Classic bun
All-beef or beef and pork hot dog
Yellow mustard
Coleslaw (store-bought or from scratch, page 152)
Chopped or sliced white onions, optional

Kitchen Notes: The type of chili used on this dog varies across West Virginia. In some counties it's a hearty, thick, spicy meat chili; in others it's more sweet than spicy. Use your favorite store-bought variety or try the recipe on page 153. You can't go wrong with any all-beef or mixed-meat hot dog. Most Slaw Dogs are made with a creamy coleslaw, though vinegar-based slaw has its merits. For homemade hot dog ingredients, see page 127.

PREP: Warm store-bought chili or prepare homemade chili according to the recipe and keep warm.

ASSEMBLY: Get out a classic bun. Grill or steam an all-beef or beef and pork hot dog (see pages 16 and 20). Place the hot dog in the bun. Add a line of yellow mustard and a pile of chili. Top with as much coleslaw as the dog will hold and a handful of onions.

Hot Dog Heaven: The annual West Virginia Hot Dog Festival in Huntingdon features all kinds of crazy dog-themed events, including an eating contest, a Bun Run 5K, and a Wiener Dog Race for more than 100 dachshunds.

HOT DOGS ON THE MAP: THE SLAW LINE

Who cares about the Mason–Dixon line? The "slaw line" runs across the very top of West Virginia, from Sistersville to Elkins. Below it—in most of the state and the rest of the South—slaw dogs are the norm. Just north of the line, coleslaw is available as an optional topping. Request a slaw dog any farther north, and chances are people won't know what you're talking about.

CORN DOG

Place of Origin: HOTLY CONTESTED ★ Other Names: CORNY DOG, COZY DOG

IN MY HOME STATE OF TEXAS, THE CORN DOG IS SAID TO HAVE BEEN INVENTED in the late 1930s by Carl and Neil Fletcher, making its debut at the annual Texas State Fair. But it wouldn't be a true American dog if its origin and creators weren't the subject of debate. Vendors at the Minnesota state fair, a drive-in in Illinois, a hot dog stand in California, and a food columnist named Sylvia Schur are among those who've claimed credit for this deep-fried dog on a stick.

**Corn Dog Batter
(page 135)**
**Barbecue stick or bamboo
skewer**
All-beef hot dog
Ketchup, optional
Mustard, optional

PREP: Make the corn dog batter according to the recipe.

ASSEMBLY: Slide a stick into an all-beef hot dog and dip the dog in the batter to coat. Deep-fry for about 5 minutes, or until golden brown. (For more on deep-frying, see page 18.) Remove to a paper towel to drain. Top with ketchup, mustard, both, or neither.

> **FUNNEL CAKE DOG:** Replace corn dog batter with waffle batter. (For a recipe, see page 135). Deep-fry the dog in vegetable oil heated to 375°F for 5 to 8 minutes, or until golden brown and crispy.
>
> **BEER BATTER DOG:** Substitute corn dog batter with beer batter. For a recipe, see page 135.
>
> **CORN BRAT:** Forget the hot dog; use a cooked bratwurst instead.

WAFFLE DOG

Place of Origin: HAWAII ★ Other Names: KC WAFFLE DOG

THE WAFFLE DOG'S STORY BEGINS IN THE 1930s IN HAWAII, WHEN THE ASATO family began serving this novel treat for customers at their small shop, KC Waffle Dogs. It wasn't long before the Waffle Dog caught on in the continental United States and throughout the Pacific. To this day, the original Hawaiian version, the backyard version of suburban America, and the street-side versions of Thailand and the Philippines are all relatively similar. Street vendors in Southeast Asia typically serve them with ketchup, whereas American vendors, including those at the original Hawaiian shop, serve them plain or with a combination of ketchup, mustard, and relish. Surprisingly, these dogs are rarely served with syrup in the wild—but that's how I prefer mine.

Waffle Batter (page 135)
All-beef hot dog
Barbecue stick or bamboo skewer
Ketchup
Yellow mustard
Classic relish (store-bought or from scratch, page 161)

PREP: Preheat a waffle iron. Prepare waffle batter according to the recipe.

ASSEMBLY: Lightly butter the waffle iron or spray it with nonstick cooking spray and pour in enough batter to fill the mold (it will expand to cover the hot dog as it cooks). Place an all-beef hot dog on top of the batter. Insert skewer, if desired. Close the iron and cook until the edges of the waffle are golden brown and crisp, about 4 to 6 minutes. Remove waffle dog from iron and top with a line each of ketchup, yellow mustard, and classic relish.

RULE-BREAKING VARIATIONS

When I served these classic Waffle Dog to my friends, they asked, "Where's the syrup?" When I served them to my spice-obsessed brother, he asked, "Can I add cayenne pepper?" So I present two sacrilegious yet crowd-pleasing variations.

MAPLE SYRUP BREAKFAST DOG: Cook Waffle Dog as above, but omit condiments. Drizzle with maple syrup.

SPICY WAFFLE DOG: Prepare waffle batter as on page 135 and add ½ teaspoon black pepper and ½ teaspoon cayenne pepper. Proceed with recipe above and omit condiments. Top dog with ketchup (store-bought or from scratch, page 148).

MODERN
AMERICAN
DOGS

TEXAS BBQ DOG

DANGER DOG • Spicy Street Dog • Chicago-Style Danger Dog

Jersey Breakfast Dog • SCRAMBLED DOG • Slaw-Topped Scrambled Dog

KANSAS CITY DOG •The Real Reuben Dog • THE REAL KANSAS CITY DOG

FENWAY FRANK • Franks-and-Beans Dog • MAXWELL STREET POLISH

CHILI CHEESE DOG • Carolina Style Dog • THE VEGAN

Spicy Vegan Dog • Plain Vegan Jane • The Vegetable Dog • Autumn Dog

WASABI DOG • SEATTLE-STYLE HOT DOG

THE NOT-SO-PLAIN JANE

TEXAS BBQ DOG

CONSIDER YOURSELF WARNED: THIS HOT DOG TAKES ALL DAY TO MAKE (though technically it is not the dog but the pulled pork topping that is so time consuming). But since you can make it all on the grill, this recipe is the perfect excuse to spend a long summer day outside. As for the precise pedigree of this loaded BBQ dog—who knows? But find me a hole-in-the-wall BBQ joint in the South that doesn't serve something like this and I'd be surprised. For the style of barbecue, I took a cue from my home state, where the focus is always on the meat and never on the sauce or sides.

Pulled Pork (page 158)
Texas BBQ Sauce (store-bought or from scratch, page 146)
Baked beans
Classic bun
American beef sausage (store-bought or from scratch, page 142)

Kitchen Notes: Pulled pork takes the better part of a day to cook, so plan ahead. Texas-style barbecue sauce is available at most grocery stores, but be sure to try the recipe on page 158 if you have time. American beef sausage, sometimes called farmer's beef sausage, is heavily seasoned and often has a pungent garlic flavor that pairs well with pulled pork and barbecue sauce.

PREP: Make pulled pork and Texas barbecue sauce, if using homemade. Make baked beans according to the package instructions and keep warm.

ASSEMBLY: Get out a classic bun. Grill an American beef sausage and toast the bun on the grill (as on page 16). Place the sausage in the bun and top with a heaping pile of pulled pork and a pile of baked beans. Serve with barbecue sauce.

MIND YOUR Bs AND Qs

Texas barbecue is all about the meat. Though Texans love beef, we're not opposed to throwing in some pork, lamb, and chicken. Unless you're serving up hot dogs, the sauce is always served on the side, not on the meat.

DANGER DOG

Place of Origin: TIJUANA, MEXICO ★ Other Names: TIJUANA BACON DOG, STREET DOG

THE DANGER DOG WAS BORN IN TIJUANA IN THE 1950s, AND ITS MONIKER COMES from the dog's reputation for being sold by unlicensed street vendors using poor-quality ingredients. (Can there be a better origin story for a hot dog?) Despite its unsavory reputation, this bacon-wrapped dog has crossed the border and made a name for itself in the States, where they are typically sold and enjoyed as late-night fare after an evening on the town. New Jersey street vendors added their own twist by placing a fried egg and cheese in the bun, bridging the gap between midnight snack and breakfast fare.

Classic Hot Dog Chili (store-bought or from scratch, page 153)
Classic bun
Beef and pork dog
Sliced uncooked bacon
Finely chopped white onions

Kitchen Note: Like it's namesake city, anything goes here—this is one hot dog with no rules regarding toppings.

PREP: Warm chili if using store-bought, or prepare it from scratch and keep warm.

ASSEMBLY: Get out a classic bun. Wrap a beef and pork dog with a slice of bacon, securing it with a wooden toothpick at each end. Deep-fry the bacon-wrapped hot dog as instructed on page 18. Remove and discard toothpicks. Place the dog in the bun and top with a heaping pile of chili and a handful of chopped onions.

You can find Danger Dogs or Street Dogs with just about anything on 'em. Try chili, fried peppers, and onions for a **SPICY STREET DOG**, sauerkraut and mustard for an homage to classic dogs, or pickles, tomatoes, onions, relish, and sport peppers for a **CHICAGO-STYLE DANGER DOG.**

JERSEY BREAKFAST DOG: Wrap an all-beef hot dog in bacon and deep-fry it as above (remember to remove the toothpicks before serving). While the hot dog is cooking, fry an egg in a small skillet. Place the egg and a slice or two of American cheese on the bun, and top with the deep-fried hot dog.

SCRAMBLED DOG

TWO DINERS IN COLUMBUS, GEORGIA—NU-WAY WIENERS AND DINGLEWOOD Pharmacy—claim to have invented this loaded, spicy dog as early as World War II, probably as the South's answer to the chili dog. In its classic form, it is topped with chili, mustard, ketchup, onions, pickles, and oyster crackers. Sometimes you'll find coleslaw offered as a topping option as well.

Spicy Bean Chili (page 153)
Classic bun
Beef and pork hot dog
Yellow mustard
Ketchup
Finely chopped white onions
Pickle slices
Oyster crackers

Kitchen Notes: Spicy bean chili can be homemade or store-bought. See From-Scratch Ingredients, page 127, if you'd like to make your own classic buns, beef and pork franks, and condiments.

PREP: Prepare spicy bean chili according to the recipe, or warm store-bought chili until hot.

ASSEMBLY: Get out a classic bun. Panfry a beef and pork hot dog on a flattop, as on page 17. Place the dog in the bun. Add a line each of yellow mustard and ketchup. Top with a heaping pile of chili, a handful of chopped onions, and a scattering of pickles slices and oyster crackers.

Locals serve it in a long bowl, banana-split-style.

SLAW-TOPPED SCRAMBLED DOG: Add a pile of coleslaw on top. (Use your favorite store-bought slaw or try the recipe on page 152.)

KANSAS CITY DOG

Place of Origin: UNKNOWN ★ Other Names: THE REUBEN DOG

A SORT OF WIENER HOMAGE TO THE REUBEN SANDWICH, THE KANSAS CITY Dog is yet another all-American creation with nebulous origins: like the Texas Dog and Coney Island Hot Dog, it is named for a place where it wasn't created. It's most likely the misnomer comes from the popularity of the Reuben sandwich in Kansas City—and the fact that the Kansas City Dog has been sold at Kauffman Stadium, home of the Kansas City Royals, for some time. The only thing hot dog historians know for sure? It's tasty.

Sesame seed bun
All-beef hot dog
Brown mustard
Swiss cheese
Sauerkraut
Caraway seeds

Kitchen Note: Sesame seed buns, all-beef hot dogs, and brown mustard can be store-bought or homemade (page 127).

PREP: Preheat a broiler.

ASSEMBLY: Get out a sesame seed bun. Panfry an all-beef hot dog on a flattop (as on page 17). Place the hot dog in the bun and smear with brown mustard. Place a couple slices of Swiss cheese on top and put the dog on a baking sheet. Broil the dog until cheese is melted, 1 to 2 minutes. Top with a pile of sauerkraut and a sprinkling of caraway seeds.

Caraway has an assertive earthy, peppery taste that's the key to many cabbage dishes, rye bread, and—with other herbs, spices, and citrus—the Scandinavian spirit aquavit. Because of their assertive flavor and medicinal uses, caraway seeds were one of Europe's first condiments (appearing in cookbooks as early as the 12th century). You can't make authentic Kansas City Dogs without them.

THE REAL REUBEN DOG: Although regular Kansas City Dogs are often called Reuben Dogs, you can make a true Reuben variation by replacing the brown mustard with Thousand Island dressing.

THE REAL KANSAS CITY DOG

Place of Origin: KANSAS CITY, MO ★ Other Names: DOG NUVO'S KC DOG

UNLIKE THE PREVIOUS HOT DOG, THIS ONE DOES HAIL FROM THE CITY FROM which it takes its name. The story goes that it's from the old KC favorite Dog Nuvo, but it can be found at diners and hot dog joints across the city, slathered in the region's signature sweet and sticky barbecue sauce.

Kansas City BBQ Sauce (store-bought or from scratch, page 147)
Classic bun
All-beef hot dog
Burnt ends (see note)
Bread and butter pickle slices

Kitchen Notes: This is a true home-style hot dog. The sauce, buns, and hot dogs can be homemade if desired (see page 127). Burnt ends are chopped-up pieces of meat cut from the ends of brisket or other barbecued meats. Save them after dinner and make Kansas City Dogs the next day, or invite friends over and serve both brisket and dogs at a massive barbecue picnic.

PREP: Prepare Kansas City barbecue sauce, or use store-bought.

ASSEMBLY: Get out a classic bun. Grill an all-beef hot dog as instructed on page 16. Place the dog in the bun. Top with a handful of burnt ends, a slathering of barbecue sauce, and a handful of pickle slices.

HOT DOGS IN HISTORY: BREAKFAST OF CHAMPIONS

Hot dogs have been fueling American innovation for decades. The last food eaten by Charles Lindbergh before his famous transatlantic flight was none other than a humble hot dog—which newspapers quickly pooh-poohed as "plebian."

FENWAY FRANK

Place of Origin: FENWAY PARK, BOSTON ★ Other Names: FENWAY PARK HOT DOG

THIS SIMPLE DOG MAY SEEM BORING STACKED ALONGSIDE SOME OF THE other dogs in this book, but as one of the first to flout the no-ketchup rule, it's worth mentioning. Not only does the Fenway Frank proudly wear ketchup, it also sports an oversized wiener inside a classic 6-inch bun, adding a lot of meaty flavor. This dog's been around the Red Sox for longer than most dogs have existed. Looking for something piled high with a local specialty? Try the Franks-and-Beans Dog, pictured (pictured, variation below) for a Beantown treat.

Classic bun
Extra-long all-beef hot dog
Yellow mustard
Ketchup

Kitchen Note: All the Fenway Frank's ingredients—including the extra-long hot dog—are tasty when homemade (using recipes, page 127), but for this ballpark dog, store-bought ingredients are more authentic. If you can't find extra-long all-beef hot dogs at the grocery story, visit your local butcher or see Sources (page 162).

ASSEMBLY: Get out a classic bun. Simmer an extra-long all-beef hot dog as instructed on page 19. Place the dog in the bun. Top with a long line of yellow mustard and ketchup.

"A HOT DOG AT THE BALLPARK BEATS ROAST BEEF AT THE RITZ." —Humphrey Bogart

FRANKS-AND-BEANS DOG: Add a heaping pile of warm baked beans to the finished dog.

MAXWELL STREET POLISH

LIKE THE HALF-SMOKE OF WASHINGTON, D.C. (SEE PAGE 53), THIS DOG IS MADE with a sausage rather than a frankfurter. Younger than other Windy City dogs, the Maxwell Street Polish came into being around the era of World War II at Jim's Original Hot Dog Stand. Proprietor Jimmy Stefanovic came up with the combination of Polish sausage and cooked onions and peppers and named the dog after the Maxwell Street Market district where his stand was located. The use of a thick, smoked sausage instead of the typical small hot dog wiener set this dog miles apart from the competition. This Polish-born sausage hitched a ride to America along with immigrants, and the onion and garlic heavy flavors managed to make kielbasa stand out among the German sausages.

Classic bun
Polish sausage
Finely chopped
    white onions
Yellow mustard
Sport peppers, optional

Kitchen Note: See page 31 for more information about sport peppers. To make from-scratch Polish sausage, see page 141.

ASSEMBLY: Get out a classic bun. Panfry a Polish sausage on a flattop (see page 17 for instructions); meanwhile, place onions alongside sausage and cook, stirring, until soft and translucent, about 8 minutes. Place the sausage in the bun. Top with a smear of yellow mustard and a pile of onions. Add a few sport peppers as well, if you like.

CHILI CHEESE DOG

Place of Origin: SOUTHWESTERN UNITED STATES ★ Other Names: CHILI DOG

UNLIKE THE PLETHORA OF CONEY DOGS IN THE NORTHEAST AND MIDWEST, this cheese-topped dog, most popular in California, Arizona, and Texas, is usually sold without mustard or onions. The chili is spicy; it's truer to Texas and Mexican chilies than the Greek-inspired meat sauces favored in the north. And like everything else in the South, it's loaded with cheese.

Spicy Southwest Chili (page 153)
Classic bun
Beef and pork hot dog
Shredded cheddar cheese

PREP: Make spicy Southwest chili according to the recipe.

ASSEMBLY: Get out a classic bun. Simmer a beef and pork hot dog (page 19). Place the hot dog in the bun. Top with as much chili and cheese as the dog can hold.

> **CAROLINA STYLE DOG:** Replace the chili with Spicy Bean Chili (page 153). Omit the cheese, and after the chili, top with a heaping pile of coleslaw (page 152) and a handful of finely chopped white onions.

THE VEGAN

Place of Origin: WESTERN UNITED STATES ★ Other Names: NOT DOG, VEGGIE DOG

IF YOU'RE VEGAN AND HAVE SOMEHOW MADE IT THROUGH ALL THE TALK ABOUT the virtues of various meaty products and natural casings, I applaud you. This recipe is your reward. Meatless sausages are almost as old as the hot dog itself, and today's vegan hot dogs are much healthier and far more flavorful than the bland not-dogs of yesteryear. Many companies sell vegan hot dogs and sausages, and almost all hot dog restaurants—especially on the West Coast—offer a vegan or vegetarian dog. Vegan wieners come in a variety of styles, using different ingredients as the base. Soy dogs are the most popular and often easiest to find. In fact, you'll likely find soy beans in tofu-based dogs and as filler in some cheaper meat-based hot dogs. Adding tomato, alfalfa sprouts, and cucumber or other fresh veggies gives this meatless dog a bright, vegetable garden flavor.

Arugula Pesto (store-bought or from scratch, page 160)
Vegan Mayonnaise (store-bought or from scratch, page 149)
Classic bun
Soy hot dog
Tomato wedges
Alfalfa sprouts
Mushroom slices
Cucumber slices

Kitchen Notes: Arugula pesto and vegan mayo are readily available in the condiments or organic-foods aisle of most supermarkets. Vegan hot dog buns are sold in many grocery stores; the classic hot dog bun recipe on page 129 happens to be vegan. For where to purchase soy dogs, see page 162.

PREP: Make arugula pesto and vegan mayonnaise according to the recipes, if using homemade.

ASSEMBLY: Get out a classic bun. Steam a soy hot dog as instructed on page 20. Place it in the bun and top it with a smear each of arugula pesto and vegan mayo. Add a few tomato wedges, a handful of alfalfa sprouts, and several mushroom and cucumber slices.

SPICY VEGAN DOG: Steam soy dog as above, but smear it with spicy mustard and top with an assortment of sliced bell peppers, jalapeños, and chiles.

PLAIN VEGAN JANE: Omit all toppings and use your favorite vegan condiments—or nothing at all!

THE VEGETABLE DOG: Replace the soy dog with a whole roasted carrot. Spread pesto and mayo on a nutty whole-grain hot dog bun, assemble the dog, and top with cooked onions and roasted cauliflower.

AUTUMN DOG: Eighty-six everything except the bun. Replace the hot dog with cooked butternut squash cubes. Top with mashed sweet potatoes, a drizzle of maple syrup, and a dusting of ground cinnamon, nutmeg, and cardamom.

MODERN AMERICAN DOGS

WASABI DOG

Place of Origin: HOUSTON, TX ★ Other Names: HAPPY ENDINGS DOG, SPICY JAPA DOG

LIKE MOST JAPANESE-INSPIRED HOT DOGS, THIS COMBINATION OF WASABI and dog comes not from Japan, but from the States . . . though not the states you might expect. Where most fusion dogs came from the Pacific Northwest, this particular spicy fusion wiener comes from deep down in Texas. Despite being a relative newcomer, it has lost its origins amid the burgeoning fusion-dog trend among restaurants, food trucks, and stands that swamped the United States in the early 2000s. Today you can find just about any Japanese ingredient mixed in and the dogs are in nearly every city. This particular Wasabi Dog recipe is inspired by a food truck, Happy Endings, in Houston, Texas. The use of a Hawaiian roll gives it a sweet bite that pairs nicely with the salty, savory sauces.

Wasabi Mayonnaise (store-bought or from scratch, page 149)
Katsu sauce
Hawaiian sweet roll
All-beef hot dog
Katsuobushi or bonito flakes
Sliced nori

Kitchen Notes: You can find recipes for Hawaiian sweet rolls and all-beef hot dogs starting on page 127. Katsuobushi are dried fish flakes made from skipjack tuna; they can be expensive, but bonito flakes are an affordable alternative. Nori is edible seaweed sold in dried sheets that can be sliced into strips and piled on top of this dog.

PREP: Make wasabi mayonnaise and katsu sauce, if using homemade.

ASSEMBLY: Get out a Hawaiian sweet roll. Grill an all-beef hot dog as instructed on page 16. Place the hot dog in the roll. Top with a smear of wasabi mayo, a line of katsu sauce, a sprinkle of katsuobushi, and a handful of seaweed strips.

Pair this dog with Wasabi Fries (page 154)— if you can handle the heat!

Katsu sauce is a sweet and tangy condiment traditionally made with applesauce, tomatoes, carrots, onions, spices, and soy sauce.

SEATTLE-STYLE HOT DOG

Place of Origin: SEATTLE, WA ★ Other Names: CREAM CHEESE DOG

THIS STRANGE SEATTLE CREATION LIKELY CAME TO BE IN THE 1980s OR '90s when modern variations and the idea of haute dogs began influencing recipes. Not only are these dogs almost impossible to find outside Seattle, they can be tricky to find within Seattle as well. That hasn't stopped this deliciously spicy and creamy dog from collecting a cult following. Loaded with veggies, jalapeños, sriracha, and cream cheese, these dogs are all about thinking outside the bun.

Oil, for sautéing

Finely chopped white onions

Sliced jalapeños

Chopped cabbage

Classic bun

Polish sausage or hot dog

Cream cheese, room temperature

Sriracha

Kitchen Notes: Anything goes! Use Polish sausage (kielbasa) or a hot dog of your choice. Originally from Vietnam, sriracha is a bright red hot sauce that's skyrocketed to fame in recent years. It's available at most grocery stores and other sources (page 162).

PREP: Warm a splash of oil in a skillet over medium heat. Add onions, jalapeños, and cabbage and cook, stirring, until they begin to soften and brown, about 10 minutes.

ASSEMBLY: Get out a classic bun. Slice a Polish sausage or hot dog in half and grill it (as in the Flattop Method for Split Dogs on page 17). Spread enough cream cheese on the inside of the bun to coat and place the sausage on top. Top with a handful of onions, jalapeños, and cabbage. Add a few drops of sriracha on top.

Let cream cheese come to room temperature before spreading so that it glides smoothly onto the bun.

THE NOT-SO-PLAIN JANE

Place of Origin: NEW YORK CITY ★ Other Names: THE $$$ DOG

REMEMBER THE HO-HUM (BUT OH SO DELICIOUS) PLAIN JANE DOG (PAGE 27)? This is her evil twin sister, hell-bent on spending the family fortune. Sink your teeth into this over-the-top juicy, plump, spicy mustard dog and you won't mind that it cost a cool hundred bucks.

Rich brioche bun
Wagyu beef hot dog
Charroux mustard
**Edible gold leaf flakes,
    optional**

Kitchen Notes: Save your pennies for this dog—not just any old bun, wiener, or mustard will do. Wagyu is a breed of cow that produces deliciously marbled beef. Charroux mustard is pungent and textured, prepared according to a decades-old family recipe. It adds a wonderfully unique bite to this dog. Edible gold leaf may not be known for its flavor, but it sure does add sparkle. These ingredients will require some searching; for Sources, see page 162.

ASSEMBLY: Get out a brioche bun. Cook a wagyu beef hot dog on a flattop according to the instructions; in the last minute or so of cooking, lightly toast the bun on the flattop (see page 17). Place the dog in the bun and top with a smear of mustard. Sprinkle with edible gold flakes if desired.

SOUTH
AND
CENTRAL
AMERICAN
DOGS

SÃO PAOLO POTATO DOG · Rio de Janeiro Dog

Paraíba Dog · Minas Gerais Dog · THE CAMPINAS DOG

EL COMPLETO · Dinámico · Chorrillana (aka Salchipapas Dog)

COLOMBIAN PINEAPPLE DOG · ECUADORIAN STREET DOG

South American Style · LOADED GUATEMALAN MEAT DOG

SÃO PAOLO POTATO DOG

Place of Origin: SÃO PAOLO, BRAZIL ★ Other Names: CACHORRO QUENTE COMPLETO

IF YOU'RE LOOKING FOR THE CRAZIEST HOT DOG IN THE WORLD, YOU'LL likely find it in Brazil. Brazilians take their toppings seriously, and though favorite add-ons vary from city to city and region to region, you'll almost always find potato on the hot dogs here. The *cachorro quente* (pronounced *ka-SHO-ho KEN-tche*, which translates simply as "hot dog") is one you'll find at street carts across São Paolo. Try it *completo*, with everything, but be warned: it won't be easy to get your hands (or mouth) around!

Mashed potatoes
Vinaigrette (store-bought or from scratch, page 160)
Canned or frozen yellow corn
Canned or frozen peas
Classic bun
Beef and pork hot dog
Ketchup
Yellow mustard
Mayonnaise
Chopped tomatoes
Potato chips
Grated cheddar cheese

Kitchen Note: See page 127 for recipes for classic buns, beef and pork hot dogs, condiments, and vinaigrette.

PREP: Make mashed potatoes and set aside, keeping warm if necessary. Whisk together the vinaigrette, if using homemade. Heat the corn and peas until hot according to the instructions on the package.

ASSEMBLY: Get out a classic bun. Grill a beef and pork hot dog as instructed on page 16. Coat the inside of the bun with mashed potatoes and place the hot dog on top. Top the dog with a line each of ketchup, yellow mustard, and mayonnaise. Add a handful each of corn, peas, tomatoes, potato chips, and cheddar cheese and finish with a spoonful or two of vinaigrette.

RIO DE JANEIRO DOG: Eighty-six the mashed potatoes and add a hardboiled quail egg.

PARAÍBA DOG: Eighty-six the mashed potatoes, potato chips, and peas. Top with potato sticks or crispy shoestring fries.

MINAS GERAIS DOG: Eighty-six the mashed potatoes and peas. Top with a mixture of cooked ground beef, carrots, red peppers, green peppers, and onions. (Minas Gerais is a Brazilian state known for its distinctive take on the Cachorro Quente.)

THE CAMPINAS DOG

Place of Origin: CAMPINAS, BRAZIL ★ Other Names: CACHORRO QUENTE DE CAMPINAS

CONTINUING BRAZIL'S REPUTATION FOR THE MOST TOPPINGS-LADEN, CRAZIEST dogs is the *cachorro quente* from the region of Campinas. The combination of ingredients may be unexpected but trust me, this a delicious dog.

Mashed potatoes
Canned or frozen corn
Canned or frozen peas
Large presliced hamburger bun
2 all-beef sausages
Mayonnaise
Ketchup
Yellow mustard
Grated cheddar cheese
Pico de gallo
Vinaigrette
Shoestring potatoes

Kitchen Notes: The hamburger bun, all-beef sausages, condiments, and vinaigrette can be homemade using the recipes that start on page 127. Also known as salsa fresca, pico de gallo is a salsa made with fresh, uncooked ingredients.

PREP: Make mashed potatoes and set aside, keeping warm if necessary. Heat the corn and peas until hot according to the instructions on the package.

ASSEMBLY: Cut a presliced hamburger bun in half, reserving one half for another use. Panfry two all-beef sausages on a flattop as instructed on page 17. Place the sausages in the halved hamburger bun. Top with a line each of mayonnaise, ketchup, and yellow mustard and a handful each of cheddar cheese, corn, and peas. Sprinkle a handful of shoestring potatoes on top. Cram a heaping pile of mashed potatoes into the bun and swipe the dull end of a knife across the top so the mashed potatoes are level with the bun. Add a spoonful each of pico de gallo and vinaigrette.

EL COMPLETO

Place of Origin: CHILE ★ Other Names: COMPLETO ITALIANO

IT'S NO MISTAKE THAT *COMPLETO* (PRONOUNCED *COM-PLAY-TO*) TRANSLATES as "complete." In Chile, frankfurters are topped to the brim with a range of condiments and ingredients, including avocado, potatoes, sauerkraut, various sauces, and more. These loaded dogs come in myriad variations, all of which put many of North America's dogs to shame. Still, it's a bit tamer than some of Brazil's dogs (see pages 89 and 90).

Classic bun
Beef and pork hot dog
Sauerkraut
Mashed avocado
Chopped tomatoes
Mayonnaise

Kitchen Note: See recipes starting on page 127 if you'd like to make your own bun, beef and pork dog, or mayonnaise.

ASSEMBLY: Get out a classic bun. Panfry a beef and pork hot dog on a flattop and toast the bun alongside it; see instructions on page 17. Place the hot dog in the bun and top with a handful of sauerkraut, a pile of mashed avocado, a spoonful or two of chopped tomatoes, and a lot of mayonnaise.

DINÁMICO: To the dog, add a smear of sauce américaine, a French sauce made with the meat, shells, or stock of a lobster. You can find it in most grocery stores or at several sources listed on page 162.

CHORRILLANA (aka Salchipapas Dog): Eighty-six all toppings. Top with a heaping pile of french fries, a handful of hot dogs sliced into $\frac{1}{2}$-inch rounds, sliced onions, a fried egg, ketchup, and mayonnaise.

¿Cómo se dice "hot dog guy" en español? In Spanish, a hot dog vendor is known as a hotdoguero.

COLOMBIAN PINEAPPLE DOG

Place of Origin: COLOMBIA ★ Other Names: COLOMBIAN HOT DOG

MEET THE *PERRO CALIENTE* (PRONOUNCED *PAIR-RO CAHL-YEN-TAY*); THE name translates literally as "hot dog." This souped-up dog is piled high with a big heap of potato chips and cheddar cheese, which add a delicious crunch.

Salsa Golf (page 159)
Pineapple Relish
  (store-bought or
  from scratch, page 161)
Classic bun
Beef and pork hot dog
Ketchup
Yellow mustard
Grated cheddar cheese
Crumbled potato chips

Kitchen Notes: Salsa golf is a sauce made with mayonnaise and ketchup; it is often flavored with spices and herbs, which vary by region. It can be found at many grocery stores in the southwestern United States, or you can make it in a jiffy using the recipe on page 159. Pineapple relish is also available in stores, but it's particularly good when freshly made, as on page 161.

PREP: Make salsa golf and pineapple relish according to the recipes, if using homemade.

ASSEMBLY: Get out a classic bun. Panfry a beef and pork hot dog on a flattop as instructed on page 17, and place the dog in the bun. Spread a line each of ketchup and yellow mustard on the dog. Add a spoonful or two each of salsa golf and pineapple relish, a handful of cheddar cheese, and a sprinkling of crumbled potato chips.

ECUADORIAN STREET DOG

Place of Origin: ECUADOR ★ Other Names: ECUADOR DOG

THE HOT DOGS YOU FIND IN ECUADOR, MOSTLY FROM STREETSIDE CARTS, are heavily sauced and flavorful affairs, thanks to a savory treatment in a garlicky water bath. Salsa verde and ají sauce give this wiener a bit of spice—and are likely to make a big ol' mess.

Salsa Verde (store-bought or from scratch, page 160)
Spicy Ají Sauce (store-bought or from scratch, page 152)
Classic bun
All-beef hot dog
Ketchup
Mayonnaise
Yellow mustard
Chopped cilantro leaves, for garnish

Kitchen Notes: Ají sauce is a spicy Peruvian condiment made with tomatoes, cilantro, ají peppers, and onions. Your favorite hot sauce will work in a pinch. Note that to prepare the Ecuadorian Water Bath, which adds loads of flavor to this dog, you will need 5 garlic cloves, a handful each of chopped tomatoes and chopped onions, and hot sauce to taste.

PREP: Make salsa verde and ají sauce according to the recipes, if using homemade.

ASSEMBLY: Get out a classic bun. Prepare an Ecuadorian Water Bath according to the instructions on page 19. Simmer an all-beef hot dog in the water bath. Place the dog in the bun and top with a line each of ketchup, mayonnaise, and yellow mustard. Add a couple spoonfuls of salsa verde and ají sauce. Sprinkle with chopped cilantro.

SOUTH AMERICAN STYLE: Add a handful of crushed potato chips to the top of the dog.

LOADED GUATEMALAN MEAT DOG

Place of Origin: GUATEMALA ★ Other Names: *SHUCO*, GUATEMALAN HOT DOG

GUATEMALA'S CONTRIBUTION TO THE TOPPINGS-CRAZY DOGS OF SOUTH AND Central America's pantheon of toppings-crazy dogs, the *shuco* is a monstrosity packed with slices of ham, bacon, pepperoni, and spicy chorizo and longaniza sausage. It may resemble a subway sandwich more than anything else, but because a wiener is buried in there somewhere, I think it's fine to call it a haute dog.

Extra-long bun (store-bought or from scratch, page 130)
Guacamole (store-bought or from scratch, page 157)
All-beef hot dog
Mayonnaise
Tomato sauce
Yellow mustard
Hot sauce
Boiled cabbage
Sliced ham
Cooked bacon strips
Sliced pepperoni
Chorizo
Longaniza

Kitchen Note: The bun, wiener, and all condiments necessary for this dog can be made at home or purchased (see Sources, page 162).

PREP: Prepare extra-long buns, guacamole, and other from-scratch ingredients, if using homemade. Panfry the chorizo and longaniza on a flattop until cooked through to 165°F, or about 10 minutes.

ASSEMBLY: Cut an extra-long classic bun lengthwise into two equal halves. Slice an all-beef hot dog in half and panfry on a flattop as instructed on page 17. Place a slice of ham, a couple strips of bacon, a few slices of pepperoni, and a 6-inch link each of chorizo and longaniza in the bun. Add the dog. Top with a smear each of mayonnaise, tomato sauce, yellow mustard, and hot sauce and a pile each of guacamole and boiled cabbage. Attempt to smash the bun closed before eating.

Know Your Meats: Chorizo and longaniza are two Spanish pork sausages made with paprika, garlic, black pepper, and other spices and are typically sold dry cured. You can find both in most grocery stores and your local butcher or international food store; in a pinch, substitute spicy Italian sausage, though it will add a fennel flavor. Vegan (soy-based) adaptations can be found at Trader Joe's and other specialty food stores.

EUROPEAN, AFRICAN, AND ASIAN DOGS

THE DANISH HOT DOG · Bacon-Wrapped Rød Pølse

The Pylsur · THE NORWEGIAN · Loaded Norwegian Dog

SWEDISH SHRIMP DOG · CZECH-STYLE SAUSAGE IN ROLL

BAGUETTE DOG · Gruyère Dog · Brie Dog

SPICY SOUTH AFRICAN SAUSAGE ROLL · GERMAN THREE-IN-A-BUN

AUTHENTIC BRATWURST · SPICY THAI DOG

THAI-STYLE FRIED DOG · Filipino Stick Dog · FRENCH FRY DOG

CHUTNEY DOG · Veggie Chutney Dog

THE DANISH HOT DOG

Place of Origin: DENMARK ★ Other Names: *RØD PØLSE, PØLSER*

DENMARK SURE DOES LOVE HOT DOGS AND HAS FOR A LONG TIME. IN FACT,
pølsevogns (translates as "hot dog carts") have been making the rounds since the early 20th
century. Although Danes may be more obsessed with hot dogs than Americans are, their dogs are
a little different from ours. The sausage, or *rød pølse* (Danish for "red sausage"), is much longer
and redder (thanks to the addition of carmine, a food coloring) than a typical frankfurter, and the
meat of the matter is finely ground pork. To hold that extra-long red sausage, the Danish prefer a
standard bun, letting the sausage hang out on both ends.

Rémoulade (page 159)
**Crunchy Fried Onions
    (store-bought or from
    scratch, page 156)**
Classic bun
**Foot-long red pork
    sausage (*rød pølse*)**
Yellow mustard
Ketchup
Diced white onion
Sliced sour pickles

*Kitchen Notes: Rød pølse
is a foot-long red pork
sausage. Although difficult
to find in the States,
your local butcher may
be able to source them.
Online vendors are listed
in Sources, page 162. The
classic bun, condiments,
and crunchy fried onions
can all be made from
scratch; see the recipes
beginning on page 127.*

PREP: Make rémoulade and crunchy fried onions, if using
homemade.

ASSEMBLY: Get out a classic bun. Panfry a foot-long red
pork sausage on a flattop (for more on this cooking method,
see page 17). Place the sausage in the bun and top with a
smear each of yellow mustard, ketchup, and rémoulade. Add
a pile each of crunchy fried onions, diced white onions, and
pickle slices on top.

BACON-WRAPPED RØD PØLSE: Wrap the pork hot
dog with a strip of bacon, securing it at both ends with
wooden toothpicks. Panfry on a flattop as instructed
on page 17. Serve on a plate with ketchup, mustard,
rémoulade, and an unsliced hot dog bun on the side.

THE PYLSUR: Eighty-six the mustard, ketchup, fried
onions, diced onions, and pickles. Top with *pylsusinnep*,
a spicy brown Icelandic mustard, or use the spicy brown
mustard of your choice.

THE NORWEGIAN

PØLSE I LOMPE (PRONOUNCED *PULSE-UH EE LOMPER* OR *LOOMPER*; TRANSLATES AS "sausage in *lompe*") is Norway's take on the hot dog. Like its Scandinavian neighbor, Norway has an obsession with the hot dog, and the two share a lot of condiments and toppings. However, Norwegian hot dogs are served in *lompe*, a flour- or potato-based flat bread, instead of a typical hot dog bun.

Flat Bread (store-bought or from scratch, page 133)
Foot-long red pork hot dog (*rød pølse*)
Yellow mustard
Ketchup

Kitchen Notes: Use store-bought flat bread or see the variation on page 133 for a more traditional Danish recipe. Rød pølse is a foot-long red pork sausage popular in Denmark. For where to find it, see page 162.

PREP: Prepare flat bread according to the recipe, if using homemade.

ASSEMBLY: Panfry a foot-long red pork hot dog on a flattop as instructed on page 17. Place the hot dog in the flat bread, top with a smear each of yellow mustard and ketchup, and roll up the bread.

> **LOADED NORWEGIAN DOG:** Top hot dog with mashed potatoes, crunchy fried onions, and rémoulade before rolling up the flat bread.

SWEDISH SHRIMP DOG

Place of Origin: SWEDEN ★ Other Names: TUNNBRÖDSRULLE, SWEDISH HOT DOG

LIKE NORWAY'S *PØLSE I LOMPE*, THE TRADITIONAL HOT DOG OF SWEDEN IS served wrapped in a flat bread from which it takes its name (*tunnbröd* translates literally as "thin bread"). But that's where the similarities end. The flat bread is rolled into a cone and packed with a wild combination of fillings, which happen to include a frankfurter. It may seem strange, but everybody should try it at least once. After all, it's become a runaway hit in Sweden as late-night, post-clubbing food.

Flat Bread (store-bought or from scratch, page 133)
Pork hot dog
Mashed potatoes
Pickle Mayonnaise (page 150)
Shrimp Salad (store-bought or from scratch, page 157)
Chopped white onions
Shredded iceberg lettuce
Ketchup
Mustard

Kitchen Note: Pickle mayo, or gurkmajonnäs, is a Swedish condiment that is often served with potatoes or sausage. Though not easily found in America, it's available in international stores or through online vendors; see Sources, page 162.

PREP: Make flat bread, mashed potatoes, pickle mayo, and shrimp salad according to the recipes, if using homemade.

ASSEMBLY: Roll a flat bread into a cone shape. Panfry a pork hot dog on a flattop (page 17). Place the hot dog in the flat bread cone and fill with a heaping pile of mashed potatoes, pickle mayo, shrimp salad, chopped white onions, and shredded lettuce. Top with a smear of ketchup and mustard.

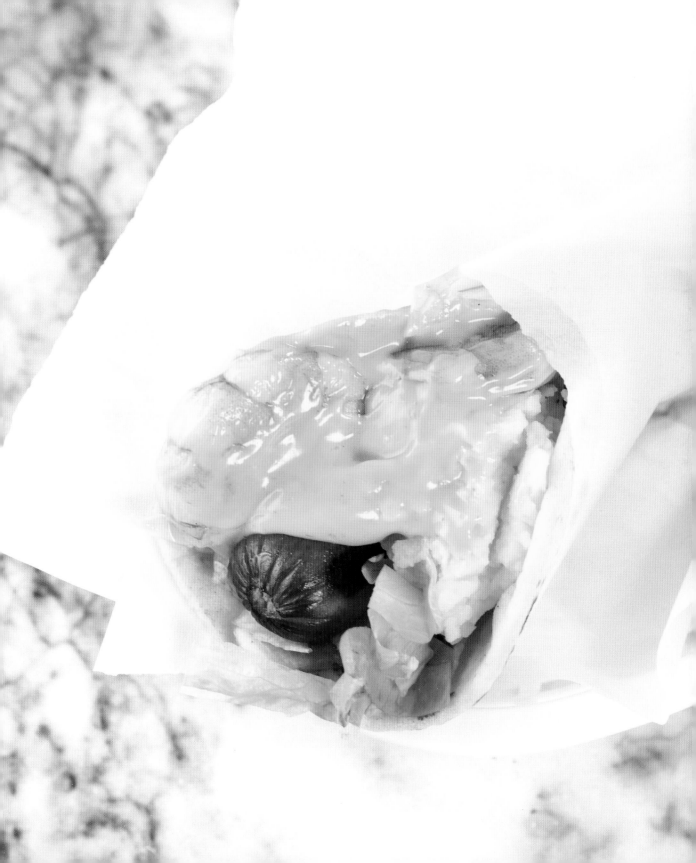

CZECH-STYLE SAUSAGE IN ROLL

Place of Origin: CZECH REPUBLIC ★ Other Names: *PÁREK V ROHLÍKU, PARKY*

PÁREK V ROHLÍKU ROUGHLY TRANSLATES AS "HOT DOG" OR LITERALLY AS "sausage in roll." It consists of a sausage and condiments—usually just a squirt of ketchup and mustard—tucked into a hollowed-out roll rather than the center of a split bun. The roll, or *rohlík*, has a thick, crispy, chewy crust, similar to a baguette.

Rohlík
Pork hot dog
Yellow mustard
Ketchup

Kitchen Notes: If you can't find rohlík, *substitute half a baguette for each wiener. Recipes for homemade pork hot dogs, yellow mustard, and ketchup begin on page 127.*

ASSEMBLY: Get out a rohlík. Using a sharp knife or clean hands, create a tunnel in the center of the length of the bread. Simmer a pork hot dog as instructed on page 19. Squirt a bit of mustard and ketchup into the hollow of the roll and then place the hot dog inside.

BAGUETTE DOG

Place of Origin: FRANCE ★ Other Names: LE HOT DOG

HOW HAS A COUNTY WITH A CUISINE KNOWN FOR METHODICAL TECHNIQUE, rich cheeses, and fine wines tackled the humble hot dog? By wrapping it in a warm, crusty baguette. French hot dog hawkers pierce their baguettes so that they toast both inside and out. You can achieve a similar effect by cutting a slit in the center and toasting the bun whole in a warm oven for a few minutes.

Short baguette
All-beef sausage
Spicy mustard
Ketchup

Kitchen Note: Beef sausage, spicy mustard, and ketchup can be homemade, if desired; see page 127.

PREP: Preheat the oven to 400°F.

ASSEMBLY: Slice the top off a short baguette and cut out a cavity through the center. Simmer an all-beef sausage as instructed on page 19; while it cooks, place the baguette in the warm oven to toast slightly. Spread a smear of spicy mustard and ketchup into the slit in the bun and slide in the sausage.

Serve this baguette dog with *frîtes*, or french fries (store-bought or from scratch, page 154).

GRUYÈRE DOG: Slice a half baguette like a classic hot dog bun and spread with spicy mustard. Eighty-six the ketchup. Add the sausage and then a generous helping of Gruyère cheese; heat under a broiler until the cheese is melted.

BRIE DOG: Follow directions for Gruyère dog, swapping Brie for Gruyère. For an extra-sweet touch, add sliced pears or apples before topping with cheese and broiling.

SPICY SOUTH AFRICAN SAUSAGE ROLL

AS THE SON OF A SOUTH AFRICAN IMMIGRANT, I AM WELL ACQUAINTED WITH THIS particular dog. *Boerewors* (pronounced *BUR-ra-vorz*; Afrikaans for "farmer's sausage") is a fatty, spicy beef-and-pork concoction served in a lightly grilled bun with a mound of sautéed onions, and a chunky, spicy, ketchup-like tomato sauce on the side. It's a typical example of the richly flavored fare of South Africa, whose culinary traditions have roots in Dutch, English, Indian, and Asian cuisines.

South African Tomato Sauce (page 148)
Vegetable oil, for sautéing
Sliced white onions
Classic bun
Boerewors (store-bought or from scratch, page 153)
Brown mustard

Kitchen Notes: A good butcher or international food store should have no trouble finding or, better yet, making boerewors for you. You can also peruse online vendors (see Sources, page 162) or make it yourself (page 153).

PREP: Prepare South African tomato sauce and sausage according to the recipes. In a skillet over medium heat, warm a splash of oil. Cook onions for 8 to 10 minutes, or until soft and light brown.

ASSEMBLY: Get out a classic bun. Grill boerewors according to the instructions on page 16; while the sausage cooks, lightly toast the bun on the grill. Place the grilled sausage in the bun. Top with a smear of brown mustard and a pile of cooked white onions. Serve with a small bowl of South African tomato sauce on the side for dipping.

GERMAN THREE-IN-A-BUN

Place of Origin: GERMANY ★ Other Names: *DREI IM WEGGLA*

DREI IM WEGGLA (PRONOUNCED *DRY IM VECK-LA*, LITERALLY "THREE IN A BREAD roll" in Nuremberg dialect) is Germany's answer to the hot dog: a trio of pork sausages served sandwich-style on a hamburger bun. The street food is found mostly in Nuremberg, and the traditional *Nürnberger Rostbratwurst* (small, thin bratwurst cooked on a grill) in the bun is made only in that city.

Hamburger bun

3 Nürnberger Rostbratwurst, or 3 small bratwursts

Spicy mustard

Kitchen Notes: Nürnberger Rostbratwurst (aka Nuremberg bratwurst) are 3- to 4-inch-long pork sausages typically seasoned with fresh marjoram. You can find these little bratwursts at your local butcher or international food store; see Sources, page 162. To make your own hamburger buns and spicy mustard, see the recipes for From-Scratch Ingredients starting on page 127.

ASSEMBLY: Slice open a hamburger bun. Grill the bratwursts as instructed on page 16. Place the sausages on the bottom of the hamburger bun. Spread a line of spicy mustard over each sausage and close the bun.

HUNGRY, HUNGRY HANS

A 16th-century German named Hans Stromer didn't let a little thing like jail time stop him from tucking into his favorite food. He allegedly ate 28,000 bratwursts during a long stay in das pokey.

AUTHENTIC BRATWURST

Place of Origin: THURINGIA, GERMANY ★ Other Names: THÜRINGER ROSTBRATWURST

THE THÜRINGER ROSTBRATWURST (PRONOUNCED *TOO-RIN-GER ROST-BRAT-vurst*, German for "Thuringian bratwurst") is a spicy pork bratwurst native to the Thuringia. It's 6 to 8 inches long—the perfect size for a bun—and typically made with garlic, caraway, and marjoram. Traditionally it is served in a roll that has been cut open, similar to a hot dog bun, and smeared with mustard and ketchup. You'll likely find many variations of this or the "three in a bun," because sausages and various rolls have been served together, if not on top of each other, for generations in Germany. The trick is knowing what to ask for in different cities and states.

Classic bun
Bratwurst, preferably
   Thuringian-style
Spicy yellow mustard

Kitchen Notes: You can find these specialty bratwursts at your local butcher or international food store, or see Sources, page 162. Recipes for classic buns and spicy yellow mustard begin on page 127.

ASSEMBLY: Get out a classic bun. Grill a bratwurst as on page 16. Place the grilled bratwurst in bun and top with a smear of spicy mustard.

RULES ARE RULES

Long before the days of the Food and Drug Administration, sausage makers were eager for their products to bear a stamp of quality. A handwritten document from 1432 forbids the use of anything but "pure, fresh pork" to make Thuringian wursts, nixing less savory ingredients like internal organs, parasites, and—oddly enough—beef.

SPICY THAI DOG

Place of Origin: THAILAND ★ Other Names: NAM CHIM DOG

THAILAND HAS AN OBSESSION WITH THE HOT DOG—CUT-UP WIENERS SHOW up there in everything from salads to pasta dishes to fried rice. When it comes to serving a dog alone, though, the Thai take is not too different from the American classic. Most vendors and restaurants serve classic hot dogs in classic buns, but instead of mustard or ketchup, you're more likely to find a sweet and spicy sauce called nam chim (Thai for "dipping sauce") coating the dog. Nam chim in Thailand is like curry in India—it's not one specific recipe, but rather a category of sauce that exists in endless variations. Most recipes start with fish sauce, lime juice, and Thai chilies and contain both sweetness and spice.

Chili nam chim (store-bought or from scratch, page 155)
Classic bun
Beef and pork hot dog

Kitchen Note: Nam chim is a Thai dipping sauce with many variations. Increase or decrease the amount of hot pepper in the recipe to suit your tastes.

PREP: Make chili nam chim according to the recipe, or use store-bought.

ASSEMBLY: Get out a classic bun. Grill or deep-fry a beef and pork hot dog (see pages 16 and 18 for more on these cooking methods). Place the hot dog in the bun and top with nam chim.

THAI-STYLE FRIED DOG

Place of Origin: THAILAND ★ Other Names: THAILAND STICK DOG

AMERICA IS NOT THE ONLY COUNTRY THAT DEEP-FRIES ITS DOGS ON A STICK. In fact, Thailand goes a step further by skipping the batter, frying a wiener bare on a stick, and then serving it with a host of sauces, including one of their nearly infinite nam chims. If you like your dogs spicy, sweet, savory, or something in between, you can find it all with this street dog on a stick.

Chili nam chim, store-bought or from scratch, (page 155)
Beef and pork hot dog
Barbecue stick or bamboo skewer

Kitchen Notes: Nam chim is a Thai dipping sauce. For a flower, pierce dog with a skewer and lay it on a flat surface. On one side, cut a slit to the skewer every 1 inch; rotate dog 90° and repeat until all sides are cut. During frying, the "petals" will open. For a spiral, pierce dog with a skewer and lay it on a flat surface. Insert a knife at a slight angle until you reach the skewer. Holding knife in place, rotate dog; stop just before the end. Stretch dog a little before frying.

PREP: Make chili nam chim according to the recipe, if using homemade.

ASSEMBLY: Slide a beef and pork hot dog onto a wooden skewer. Deep-fry the hot dog (as described on page 18) until the skin is crispy and edges begin to brown. Remove the skin and serve the hot dog either smeared with nam chim or with the sauce on the side for dipping.

Street carts in Thailand sell these dogs cut into an assortment of interesting shapes. Use a sharp knife to cut dogs into shapes such as spirals, flowers, cubes, and more that will open up during frying (see Kitchen Notes).

FILIPINO STICK DOG: Replace the beef and pork hot dog with a bright red hot dog. Eighty-six the chili nam chim and top with banana ketchup (see page 148 for a recipe).

FRENCH FRY DOG

Place of Origin: THAILAND ★ Other Names: SOUTH KOREAN CORN DOG

IF YOU LOVE CORN DOGS AND WAFFLE DOGS, YOU'LL LOVE THE POTATO-filled crisp bite of this dog on a stick. Battered dogs on sticks reign supreme in South Korea, and adding french fries to the batter—yes, you read that correctly—might just earn this version the honor of king of all battered wieners. Serve it piping hot and dip it in your favorite condiments.

**Classic Fries
    (page 154)**
**Corn Dog Batter
    (page 135)**
Beef and pork hot dog
**Barbecue stick or bamboo
    skewer**
Mustard, optional
Ketchup, optional

Kitchen Note: Feeling adventurous? Instead of french fries, try sweet potato fries, curly fries, tater tots, or hash browns.

PREP: Make fries according to the recipe, or cook store-bought fries according to the package instructions. Mix the corn dog batter according to the recipe.

ASSEMBLY: Slice the end of a beef and pork hot dog onto a wooden skewer. Dip the hot dog in the corn dog batter and then roll it in french fries. Deep-fry the dog as instructed on page 18 for about 5 to 8 minutes, until the fries are browned and crispy and the hot dog is cooked through. Serve as is or top with a line or two of mustard or ketchup.

123

EUROPEAN, AFRICAN, AND ASIAN DOGS

CHUTNEY DOG

YOU WON'T FIND MANY BEEF-AND-PORK HOT DOGS IN INDIA, WHERE COWS are considered sacred and vegetarianism is widespread. Nevertheless, many young entrepreneurs are importing new and clever twists to the streets of India. The American copycat recipes feature dogs made with halal chicken or vegetarian wieners. Tamarind paste and mango chutney add a deliciously sweet and spicy tang you won't find with other dogs.

Mango Chutney (store-bought or from scratch, page 155)
Olive oil, for sautéing
Sliced white onions
Classic bun
Chicken dog
Tamarind paste

Kitchen Notes: Want to make your own chicken dogs? See page 139. Tamarind paste is made from the tamarind fruit and commonly used to give a sweet-sour taste to Asian and Middle Eastern dishes. See Sources (page 162) for where to buy it.

PREP: Make mango chutney according to the recipe, if using homemade. In a small skillet, warm a little olive oil. Add sliced white onions and cook, stirring, until soft and translucent, about 8 minutes.

ASSEMBLY: Get out a classic bun. Panfry a chicken dog on a flattop as instructed on page 17. Place the dog in the bun. Add a dash of tamarind paste, a smear of mango chutney, and a handful of cooked onions.

Chutney is a spicy condiment made with fruits (such as mango), vinegar, sugar, and spices. A delicious accompaniment to savory foods like curried dishes and (of course!) hot dogs, it can range from chunky to smooth and from sweet and mild to bold and hot.

VEGGIE CHUTNEY DOG: Substitute a vegetarian or vegan hot dog for the chicken dog.

FROM-SCRATCH HOT DOG INGREDIENTS

BUNS AND BATTERS: Classic Hot Dog Buns
Sesame Seed Buns • Poppy Seed Buns • New England-Style Buns
Extra-Long Buns • Hamburger Buns • Rich Whole Wheat Buns
Hawaiian Sweet Bread Rolls • Flat Bread
Grill-Top Flat Bread • Potato Lompe • Corn Dog Batter
Waffle Batter • Beer Batter

HOT DOGS: WIENERS, FRANKFURTERS, AND SAUSAGES:
All-Beef Hot Dogs • Extra-Long All-Beef Hot Dogs • Wagyu Beef Hot Dogs
All-Pork Hot Dogs • Beef and Pork Hot Dogs • Pork and Veal Hot Dogs
Pork and Lamb Hot Dogs • Chicken Hot Dogs • Bratwurst
Polish Sausage (Kielbasa) • American Beef Sausage
South African Sausage (Boerewors)

CONDIMENTS, SAUCES, AND TOPPINGS: Texas BBQ Sauce
Kansas City BBQ Sauce • Carolina-Style BBQ Sauce
Memphis-Style BBQ Sauce • Quick Ketchup • Spicy Ketchup
South African Tomato Sauce • Banana Ketchup • Mayonnaise
Wasabi Mayonnaise • Vegan Mayonnaise • Pickle Mayonnaise (Gurkmajonnäs)
Yellow Mustard • Spicy Yellow Mustard • Dijon Mustard • Horseradish Mustard
Whole Grain Mustard • Brown (Deli) Mustard • Spicy Brown Mustard
Spicy Ají Sauce • Coleslaw • Katsu Sauce • Classic Hot Dog Chili • Greek Sauce
Coney Island Sauce • Tomato-Based Chili Sauce • Rhode Island Chili
Rochester Meat Sauce • Spicy Southwest Chili • Spicy Bean Chili • District Chili
Classic Fries • Fried Potato Wedges • Thick-Cut Fries • Frîtes • Wasabi Fries
Mango Chutney • Chili Nam Chim • New York Style Sautéed Onions
Crunchy Fried Onions • Guacamole • Shrimp Salad • Pulled Pork
Texas Dry Rub • Rémoulade • Salsa Golf • Salsa Verde • Vinaigrette • Arugula
Pesto • Relish • Neon Green Relish • Chili Relish • Pineapple Relish

BUNS AND BATTERS

There are many buns, breads, and dough vessels that a hot dog
can be eaten from, but none is more iconic than the classic hot dog bun.
I've included two fairly simple classic recipes here. The first is a plain bun,
with no bells or whistles, and it is as close as you can get to store-bought
without adding a bunch of preservatives and chemicals. It's light, airy,
and just chewy enough to stand up to a large wiener with tons of toppings.
The second is a heartier, more flavorful version made with milk, eggs,
and butter. Both buns are delicious, and because they bake at the same
temperature, it's easy to make a batch of each at once. In addition to
these recipes, I've included instructions for making pita bread,
flat breads, and batters for corn dogs and waffle dogs.

CLASSIC HOT DOG BUNS

WHILE WRITING THIS BOOK, I HELD BLIND TASTE TESTS WITH MY FAMILY AND friends to determine which recipes were worthy of inclusion. When it was time to test breads, I was ecstatic. I had created seven deliciously rich doughs I was sure would be crowd-pleasers. Out of mere obligation, I included a single vegan recipe, but I took little care in its preparation. To my surprise, every single friend and family member told me the vegan recipe was their favorite. To be sure it wasn't a fluke, I repeated the taste test, this time making a few more varieties of the vegan dough and taking much more care in its preparation. And once again the vegan recipe came out on top. Not only is it tasty, it's quick, simple, and cheap.

MAKES 8 BUNS

1 teaspoon active
dry yeast
2 tablespoons (1 ounce)
sugar
$1/2$ cup water, warmed
to 110°F
$1^3/_4$ cups plus 2
tablespoons ($8^1/_2$
ounces) bread flour
$1/2$ teaspoon salt
3 tablespoons ($1^1/_2$ fluid
ounces) soybean oil

*Kitchen Note: If you can't
find soybean oil in the
grocery store, simply read
the ingredients on the
labels of those available.
Most commercial vegetable
oils are 100% soybean oil.*

1. In the warm bowl of a stand mixer or a glass or metal bowl, dissolve the yeast and sugar in the warm water by stirring for 5 minutes until the liquid appears slightly foamy and no visible granules of yeast remain.

2. Add flour, salt, and soybean oil and mix by hand until a dough begins to form.

3. Using the dough hook attachment, knead dough on medium-low speed for about 8 minutes, or until smooth and elastic. Alternatively, knead by hand on a lightly floured surface until smooth and elastic.

4. Place dough in a lightly oiled bowl at least 3 times the size of the dough. Cover with a lightly floured tea towel and let rise in a warm spot (ideally around 80°F) until doubled in volume, about 2 hours.

5. Lightly press on the dough to deflate it. Fold dough in on itself a few times to redistribute yeast.

6. Divide dough into 8 equal portions. Roll each portion into a ball, place balls on a lightly floured surface, and cover with a lightly floured tea towel. Let rest for 20 minutes. While dough rests, line a 12-by-17-inch baking sheet with parchment paper and dust lightly with flour.

7. Using your hands, shape balls into individual buns. Roll each piece into a flat rectangle about 6 inches by 2 inches;

(continued)

with the long side facing you, tightly roll the dough, pinching the long ends to stretch the dough each time you roll it. Then gently tuck the exposed short ends underneath to create smooth ends and pinch the ends toward the bottom of the bun to keep them in place.

8. Arrange buns, about $3/4$ to 1 inch apart in a single line, on the prepared baking sheet. Cover with a lightly floured tea towel and let rise in a warm spot until doubled in volume (they should be touching and measure about $1^1/_2$ to 2 inches tall), about 1 hour. Meanwhile, preheat oven to 400°F.

9. When buns have doubled in volume, place baking sheet in oven. Reduce temperature to 375°F and bake for 14 to 16 minutes, or until the tops are golden brown. Let buns cool completely. Separate buns and slice each down the center, almost all the way through but leaving one side intact.

Warm Bowls: Warming a mixing bowl before mixing the dough will help keep ingredients warm so that the yeast remains active. Simply run the inside and outside of the bowl under hot water until warm to the touch. Dry thoroughly and use right away.

SESAME SEED BUNS: Just before baking, dampen your hand slightly and run it over the top of the buns. Sprinkle sesame seeds over each. Bake as instructed.

POPPY SEED BUNS: Just before baking, dampen your hand slightly and run it over the top of the buns. Sprinkle poppy seeds over each. Bake as instructed.

NEW ENGLAND-STYLE BUNS: Instead of a flat baking sheet, use a prepared 6-by-12-inch baking dish with 1-inch sides. Place buns a bit closer together than in the main recipe and let them rise until they are $1/2$ inch higher than the sides of the pan. Bake as instructed and cut through the top instead of the side.

EXTRA-LONG BUNS: Instead of dividing the dough into 8 portions, divide into quarters. Shape the buns as desired; they can be wider or longer than regular buns. Increase baking time by 2 minutes.

HAMBURGER BUNS: Double the recipe and divide the dough into 8 portions. In step 7, fold the long rectangle in half to create a square. Roll the square dough toward the center to create hamburger bun shape. Proceed as instructed

RICH WHOLE WHEAT BUNS

OF ALL THE BUNS THAT LOST TO THE TRUSTY VEGAN RECIPE, THIS IS MY personal favorite (and the recipe I use for just about every bread and roll I bake).

**MAKES 8
HOT DOG BUNS**

¹/₂ cup whole milk

1 teaspoon active
   dry yeast

2 tablespoons (1 ounce)
   sugar

1 large egg, at room
   temperature

1¹/₄ cups plus 1
   tablespoon (6 ounces)
   all-purpose flour

¹/₄ cup plus 1 tablespoon
   (2 ounces) whole wheat
   flour

³/₄ teaspoon salt

³/₄ ounce (1¹/₂
   tablespoons) unsalted
   butter, at room
   temperature

*Kitchen Note: For more on
using warm bowls—as in
step 2 of this recipe—see
the previous page.*

1. In a saucepan fitted with a thermometer, scald milk by heating it to 140°F, or until bubbles begin to form around the side of the pan and a film appears on the surface. Remove from heat and let cool to 110°F.

2. In the warm bowl of a stand mixer, or a glass or metal bowl, combine yeast and the warm milk and stir for 5 minutes, until the liquid appears slightly foamy and no visible yeast granules remain.

3. Add sugar and egg and mix by hand until the yolk breaks. Add flours, salt, and butter and mix until a dough begins to form.

4. Using the dough hook attachment, knead dough on medium-low speed for about 8 minutes, or until smooth and elastic. Alternatively, knead by hand on a lightly floured surface until smooth and elastic.

5. Place dough in a lightly oiled or buttered bowl at least 3 times the size of the dough. Cover with a lightly floured tea towel and let rise in a warm spot (ideally around 80°F) until doubled in volume, about 2 hours.

6. Lightly press on the dough to deflate it. Fold dough in on itself a few times to redistribute the yeast.

7. Divide dough into 8 equal portions. Roll each portion into a ball, place balls on a lightly floured surface, and cover with a lightly floured tea towel. Let rest for 20 minutes. While dough rests, line a 12-by-17-inch baking sheet with parchment paper and dust lightly with flour.

8. Using your hands, shape balls into individual buns. Roll each piece into a flat rectangle about 6 inches by 2 inches; with the long side facing you, tightly roll the dough,

(continued)

pinching the ends to stretch the dough each time you roll it. Then gently tuck the exposed ends underneath to create smooth ends and pinch the ends toward the bottom of the bun to keep them in place.

9. Arrange buns in a single line, about $^3/_4$ to 1 inch apart, on the prepared baking sheet. Cover with a lightly floured tea towel and let rise in a warm spot until doubled in volume (they should be touching and measure about 1$^1/_2$ to 2 inches tall), about 1 hour. Meanwhile, preheat oven to 400°F.

10. When buns have doubled in volume, place baking sheet in oven. Reduce temperature to 375°F and bake for 14 to 16 minutes, or until the tops are golden brown.

11. Remove baking sheet from oven and let buns cool completely. Separate buns and slice each down the center, almost all the way through but leaving one side intact.

HAWAIIAN SWEET BREAD ROLLS: Substitute all-purpose flour for the whole wheat flour Add 2 tablespoons ($^1/_2$ ounce) corn flour to the dough with the flour. Add 2 teaspoons ($^1/_2$ ounce) honey to the dough with the sugar and egg. Before baking, brush warm honey on the top of each bun.

FLAT BREAD

OUTSIDE THE UNITED STATES, HOT DOGS ARE NOT ALWAYS SERVED IN BUNS. Here is a delightfully simple and easy-to-make flat bread that is perfect for those not-so-American dogs.

MAKES ABOUT 8 FLAT BREADS

2¹/₄ cups (10 ounces) all-purpose flour
1 teaspoon salt
³/₄ cup water, divided

1. In a large bowl, mix together flour and salt.

2. Add half the water and mix with a wooden spoon or your hands until a stiff dough forms. Add the remaining water as needed to make a soft but not sticky dough.

3. Turn out dough onto an unfloured surface and knead for about 10 minutes. Sprinkle a little water on the dough if it becomes too dry and unworkable.

4. Place dough in a lightly oiled bowl. Cover and let rest in a warm place for 1 hour.

5. Roll dough into a rope and cut into 8 equal portions. Shape each piece into a ball and then, on a lightly floured surface, roll it out into a 6-inch disk.

6. Warm a skillet or a griddle over medium heat. Lightly oil the cooking surface. Cook disks a couple at a time for 4 to 5 minutes, or until bubbles appear in the dough. Flip and cook for another 4 to 5 minutes, until the bottom begins to brown.

7. Serve immediately or store in an airtight container at room temperature for up to 2 days. You can keep flat bread warm in an oven set to the warm setting, or about 170°F.

GRILL-TOP FLAT BREAD: Cook the flat bread on a grill set to medium-high heat for 2 to 4 minutes per side, until the bottom begins to brown.

POTATO LOMPE: Replace half the flour with ¹/₂ cup (4 ounces) mashed potatoes. Reduce water to 2 tablespoons.

CORN DOG BATTER

This quick and easy batter will give you perfect corn dogs—crispy on the outside, fluffy on the inside—that will take you back to the state fair.

MAKES ENOUGH BATTER FOR ABOUT 4 CORN DOGS

$^1/_2$ cup (2$^1/_4$ ounces) yellow cornmeal
$^1/_2$ cup (2$^1/_4$ ounces) all-purpose flour
$^1/_2$ teaspoon salt
$^1/_2$ teaspoon baking powder
$^1/_2$ teaspoon baking soda
1 large egg
$^3/_4$ cup whole milk

Combine cornmeal, flour, salt, baking powder, and baking soda in a medium bowl. In another medium bowl, combine egg and milk. Pour wet ingredients into dry ingredients and stir until a batter forms. Use immediately.

WAFFLE BATTER

Not in the mood for waffle dogs? Throw this batter on your waffle iron, get out some butter and syrup, and make breakfast instead.

MAKES ABOUT 6 WAFFLE DOGS OR 4 STANDARD WAFFLES

1 cup (5 ounces) all-purpose flour
2 tablespoons (1 ounce) sugar
$^1/_2$ teaspoon salt
1 tablespoon baking powder
1 large egg
$^3/_4$ cup whole milk
2 tablespoons (1 ounce) unsalted butter, melted
1$^1/_2$ teaspoons vanilla extract

In a large bowl, combine flour, sugar, salt, and baking powder. In another medium bowl, combine egg, milk, butter, and vanilla. Pour wet ingredients into dry ingredients and stir until a batter forms. Use immediately.

> **BEER BATTER:** Replace whole milk with beer of your choice.

HOT DOGS: WIENERS, FRANKFURTERS, AND SAUSAGES

Making your own hot dogs and sausages is one of the funnest and most satisfying processes you can do. Not only is it a blast turning simple cuts of meat, herbs, and flavorings into delicious edibles, but being able to control the flavor will leave you wondering why you ever bought sausages from the store. Invite your friends or family into the kitchen for these recipes—the extra hands will help the process fly by.

GEAR UP

You will need a few specialty tools: a meat grinder, a sausage filler, and, if you plan to smoke your sausages and hot dogs, a smoker.

FAT IN SAUSAGE

Much of the juiciness and flavor in hot dogs and sausages comes from fat. Most cuts of meat sold in grocery stores have already been trimmed of most fat, so if you'll be working with these products, you'll need to add extra fat to your sausage. I recommend calling the grocery store's butcher and asking if you can reserve the trimmed fat—it's cheap, and you can usually get it for as little as 25 cents a pound (or less!).

The Rules of Homemade Sausage

Making sausages at home may seem daunting, but if you follow these simple guidelines, it can be a carefree process with delicious results.

1. Keep ingredients and tools as cold as possible. Freeze meats and fats for 1 to 2 hours before grinding. Keep all ingredients you're not working with in the refrigerator or freezer.

2. Make sure your tools are extremely clean. Wash them with soap in hot water. Rinse well with cold water and chill in the refrigerator for a few minutes before using.

3. Rinse natural casings well to remove the packing salt before using.

4. If smoking meats, make sure you use curing salts and pay careful attention to smoking temperatures and the temperature of the final product. Sausages need to be smoked or cooked to an internal temperature of 160°F.

5. Taste before making all the sausages: After mixing the spices into the ground meat, form a small meatball or patty. Cook in a skillet pan with a little oil until it reaches an internal temperature of 160°F. Taste and then adjust seasoning as needed.

Curing Meats

Curing is necessary when making smoked hot dogs and sausages because the meats are kept at low temperatures for an extended period. This "danger zone"—between 40°F and 140°F—is where bacteria can flourish. Cures contain nitrates and nitrites, naturally occurring chemical compounds that create an environment (in these recipes, the sausages and hot dogs) that is unappealing or downright unsuitable for bacteria to survive and grow. (Oh, and about the whole nitrate/nitrite health scare, it's nothing to worry about—both compounds are found naturally in vegetables and our bodies, without the aid of a pound of bacon for breakfast.) There are many cures on the market; some are mixed with salt, others are not, so always follow the instructions on the package.

Avoiding the Danger Zone

Even though curing agents will help keep sausage and hot dogs safe from bacteria, you should still ensure that all your ingredients and tools are cold while making sausages, especially raw sausages like bratwurst (page 140). Ideally, everything should be so chilled that your hands begin to hurt after working with the meat and tools for just a few minutes. As soon as things warm enough that your hands are comfortable, it's time to return everything to the freezer. Chill for about 20 minutes, or until ice crystals form.

NATURAL CASINGS

As with trimmed fat, you can usually buy natural casings from a butcher. Different types range in size, but the typical lamb (or sheep), hog, or bovine casing will be more than long enough for dozens of sausages (you can make upwards of 100 sausages with one natural casing). I suggest hog casings for sausages and lamb casings for hot dogs. Natural casings are stored in salt, so rinse them inside and out and then soak in water for 24 hours in the refrigerator. Just before stuffing, soak casings in warm water to make them easier to work with.

ALL-BEEF HOT DOGS

BE PREPARED: MAKING HOT DOGS AT HOME IS A MESSY, TIME-CONSUMING process. The dogs must be smoked and cooked—two more steps than most sausage recipes— making the process far from quick. But if, like me, you are enamored of frankfurters, then you should try making them at least once.

MAKES 1 POUND (8 LINKS)

6 feet sheep casing
4 ounces beef flank
4 ounces beef top round
4 ounces beef chuck shoulder
4 ounces beef fat
1$^1/_2$ teaspoons curing salt, such as Morton Tender Quick
2 tablespoons finely grated onion
2 tablespoons finely chopped garlic
1 teaspoon ground ginger
$^1/_2$ teaspoon ground mustard
$^1/_8$ teaspoon ground cayenne pepper
$^1/_2$ cup ice water
Hickory wood chips, for smoking

Kitchen Notes: Curing salt—such as Morton Tender Quick—is a mixture of salt, sugar, nitrate, and nitrite (the last two are curing agents). In a pinch, substitute $^1/_4$ teaspoon Cure #1 and 1$^1/_4$ teaspoons salt. Always follow instructions on the packaging—using the wrong amount of nitrates can be dangerous.

1. Soak sheep casing in a bowl of warm water for 1 hour.

2. Chop meats and fat into 1-inch chunks, or the size indicated by the instructions for your sausage maker or meat grinder. Process meat and fat through the sausage maker fitted with the fine grinder attachment, following manufacturer's instructions.

3. Freeze mixture for 20 minutes, or until it begins to harden.

4. Reprocess mixture through sausage maker fitted with the fine grinder.

5. Transfer mixture to a large bowl and combine with curing salt, onion, garlic, ginger, ground mustard, and cayenne pepper. Freeze mixture for another 20 minutes, or until it begins to harden.

6. Process mixture a third time through sausage maker fitted with the fine grinder.

7. In the bowl of a food processor, pulse meat mixture to break it apart, and add ice water in small increments. If the bowl or meat mixture no longer feels cold, place the bowl in the freezer for 20 minutes, or until ice crystals begin to form. Mix until all the water is added and a paste is formed.

8. Attach wet casing to the tubing attachment of the sausage maker. Tie a knot at the end of the casing and poke a small hole at the end to release air.

9. Feed meat puree through sausage maker into casing, following manufacturer's instructions, letting it create a coil. Leave a foot of unfilled casing before cutting it from the machine.

10. Smooth and shape the puree in the casing so that the diameter is even throughout the coil. Every 6 inches, twist coil several times to create links. When the entire coil has been shaped and linked, knot the end and cut off excess unfilled casing.

11. Prepare a smoker according to manufacturer's instructions. Smoke hot dogs over hickory chips at 170°F for 1 to 2 hours, or until hot dogs turn dark red. (Although they look good enough to eat, smoked dogs must be steamed and fully cooked before consuming.)

12. Place a steamer insert in a pot of water and bring to a simmer. Transfer hot dogs to the steam tray. Steam for 10 minutes, or until the internal temperature of the hot dogs reaches 160°F. While the dogs cook, prepare a bowl of ice water. Transfer hot dogs to the cold water to stop the cooking. Once cool enough to handle, hang hot dogs on a rack or on hooks to air-dry in your kitchen or any dry and cool indoor environment for 2 to 3 hours, to cool completely and bloom.

13. Wrap hot dogs together in parchment paper and store in an airtight container in the refrigerator for up to 4 days, or in the freezer for up to 3 months. Heat before serving using one of cooking methods beginning on page 15.

MORE TO TRY

There's more than one way to make a hot dog. Try these popular versions or experiment with combinations of your favorite meats.

EXTRA-LONG ALL-BEEF HOT DOGS: For a foot-long dog, tie off the links every 12 inches instead of every 6 inches. This will yield 4 hot dogs.

WAGYU BEEF HOT DOGS: Use wagyu beef instead of beef (use the same cuts of meat as in the original recipe).

ALL-PORK HOT DOGS: Replace beef and beef fat with 8 ounces pork shoulder, 4 ounces pork belly, and 4 ounces pork fat.

BEEF AND PORK HOT DOGS: Halve the quantities of beef and beef fat and add 4 ounces pork shoulder, 2 ounces pork belly, and 2 ounces pork fat.

PORK AND VEAL HOT DOGS: Replace beef and beef fat with 4 ounces pork shoulder, 2 ounces pork belly, 6 ounces veal, and 4 ounces pork fat.

PORK AND LAMB HOT DOGS: Replace beef and beef fat with 4 ounces pork shoulder, 2 ounces pork belly, 6 ounces lamb shank, and 4 ounces pork fat.

CHICKEN HOT DOGS: Replace beef and beef fat with 1 pound ground chicken.

BRATWURST

BRATWURST IS A FRESH GERMAN SAUSAGE THAT IS NOT SMOKED AND RARELY sold cooked. It gets its distinctive aroma from spices like nutmeg, mace, and ginger. Use it in your favorite hot dog recipes when you crave richer flavor and spice.

MAKES 1 POUND (4 LINKS)

6 feet hog casing, soaked in warm water for 1 hour
8 ounces pork shoulder
4 ounces pork belly
4 ounces pork fat
2 tablespoons (1 fluid ounce) whole milk
1 1/2 teaspoons salt
3/4 teaspoon freshly ground black pepper
1/2 teaspoon ground nutmeg
1/4 teaspoon ground mace
1/4 teaspoon freshly grated ginger

Kitchen Note: Chop meat and fat into 1-inch chunks, or the size indicated by the instructions for your sausage maker or meat grinder.

1. Process meat and fat through a sausage maker fitted with the large grinder attachment, following manufacturer's instructions.

2. In a large bowl, gently mix ground meat with milk, salt, pepper, nutmeg, mace, and ginger until evenly distributed. Take care not to mash or tear apart the chunks of meat and fat.

3. Attach wet casing to the tubing attachment of the sausage maker. Tie a knot in the end of the casing and poke a small hole at the end to release air.

4. Feed meat mixture through sausage maker into casing, following manufacturer's instructions, letting it create a coil. Leave a foot of unfilled casing before cutting it from the machine.

5. Smooth and shape mixture in casing so that the diameter is even throughout the coil. Every 6 inches, twist coil several times to create links. When the entire coil has been shaped and linked, knot the end and cut off excess unfilled casing. Cut bratwust between each link, in the middle of the twisted casing. If the knots aren't twisted enough, the ends may unwrap when cutting.

6. Wrap bratwurst together in parchment paper and store in an airtight container in the refrigerator for up to 4 days or in the freezer for up to 3 months. Before consuming, cook to an internal temperature of 160°F using one of the cooking methods starting on page 15.

POLISH SAUSAGE (KIELBASA)

IN THE UNITED STATES, POLISH SAUSAGE, OR KIELBASA, IS OFTEN SOLD AS smoked sausage. Where hot dogs are only partially smoked and then steamed, Polish sausages are cooked by smoking alone, which gives them a distinctive flavor and rich red hue; they need only to be reheated before eating. This variety gets its distinctive flavor from marjoram and garlic.

**MAKES 1 POUND
(4 LINKS)**

6 feet hog casing, soaked in warm water for 1 hour

8 ounces pork shoulder

4 ounces pork belly

4 ounces pork fat

1¹/₂ teaspoons curing salt, such as Morton Tender Quick (see note on page 138)

³/₄ teaspoon freshly ground black pepper

1 tablespoon finely chopped garlic

1 tablespoon finely chopped marjoram

Hickory wood chips, for smoking

Kitchen Note: Chop meat and fat into 1-inch chunks, or the size indicated by the instructions for your sausage maker or meat grinder.

1. Process chopped meat through a sausage maker fitted with the large grinder attachment, following manufacturer's instructions.

2. In a large bowl, gently mix ground meat with curing salt, pepper, garlic, and marjoram until evenly distributed. Take care not to mash or tear apart the chunks of meat and fat.

3. Attach wet casing to the tubing attachment of the sausage maker. Tie a knot in the end of the casing and poke a small hole at the end to release air.

4. Feed meat mixture through sausage maker into casing, following manufacturer's instructions, letting it create a coil. Leave a foot of unfilled casing before cutting it from the machine.

5. Smooth and shape mixture in casing so that the diameter is even throughout the coil. Every 6 inches, twist coil several times to create links. When the entire coil has been shaped and linked, knot the end and cut off excess unfilled casing.

6. Prepare a smoker according to the manufacturer's instructions. Smoke sausages over hickory chips at 170°F for 3 hours, or until the internal temperature reaches 160°F.

7. Remove sausages from smoker and place in a bowl of very cold water to stop the cooking. Once cool enough to handle, hang sausages on a rack to air-dry in a dry and cool indoor environment for 2 to 3 hours, to cool completely and bloom. Wrap sausages together in parchment paper and store in an airtight container in the refrigerator for up to 4 days or in the freezer for up to 3 months. Before serving, heat sausages using one of the cooking methods starting on page 15.

AMERICAN BEEF SAUSAGE

AMERICAN BEEF SAUSAGE, OR FARMER'S SAUSAGE, CAN BE FOUND THROUGHOUT America, especially in cattle-loving states like my home turf of Texas. This recipe showcases my favorite combination of beef cuts and spices (thyme, garlic, and parsley), but you can flavor the meat with just about any spice or herb you like and experiment with different cuts as well.

MAKES 1 POUND

6 feet beef or hog casing, soaked in warm water for 1 hour

4 ounces beef flank

4 ounces beef top round

4 ounces beef chuck shoulder

4 ounces beef fat

1¹/₂ teaspoons curing salt, such as Morton Tender Quick (see note on page 138)

³/₄ teaspoon freshly ground black pepper

1 tablespoon finely chopped fresh thyme

¹/₂ tablespoon finely chopped fresh parsley

¹/₂ tablespoon finely chopped garlic (from about 1 clove)

Hickory wood chips, for smoking

Kitchen Note: Chop meat and fat into 1-inch chunks, or the size indicated by the instructions for your sausage maker or meat grinder. Most sausage makers and meat grinders are similar, but be sure to read and follow the manufacturer's instructions.

1. Process meat and fat through a sausage maker fitted with the large grinder attachment.

2. Gently mix ground meat with curing salt, pepper, thyme, parsley, and garlic. Take care not to mash or tear apart the chunks of meat and fat.

3. Attach wet casing to the tubing attachment of the sausage maker. Tie a knot in the end of the casing and poke a small hole at the end to release air.

4. Feed meat mixture through sausage maker into casing, letting it create a coil. Leave a foot of unfilled casing before cutting it from the machine.

5. Smooth and shape mixture in casing so that the diameter is even throughout the coil. Every 6 inches, twist coil several times to create links. When the entire coil has been shaped and linked, knot the end and cut off excess unfilled casing.

6. Prepare a smoker according to manufacturer's instructions. Smoke sausages over hickory chips at 170°F for 3 hours, or until the internal temperature reaches 160°F.

7. Remove sausages from smoker and place in a bowl of very cold water to stop the cooking. Once cool enough to handle, hang sausages on a rack or hooks to air-dry in any dry, cool indoor environment for 2 to 3 hours.

8. Wrap completely cooled sausages together in parchment paper and store in an airtight container in the refrigerator for up to 4 days or in the freezer for up to 3 months. Before serving, heat sausages using one of the cooking methods starting on page 15.

SOUTH AFRICAN SAUSAGE
(BOEREWORS)

I WAS RAISED ON THIS STUFF, SO I MAY BE BIASED, BUT BOEREWORS (PRO-
nounced *BUR-ra-vorz*) is my favorite sausage, especially when it's made by my South African father. Loaded with spices and flavor, this fresh beef and pork sausage is formed into a single long coil that is grilled whole and then cut to size to fit a hot dog bun.

MAKES 1 POUND

6 feet sheep or hog casing, soaked in warm water for 1 hour

2 ounces beef flank

2 ounces beef top round

2 ounces beef chuck shoulder

4 ounces pork shoulder

2 ounces pork belly

4 ounces beef or pork fat

2 teaspoons salt

1 teaspoon freshly ground black pepper

1 teaspoon ground cloves

¹/₂ teaspoon ground allspice

¹/₂ teaspoon ground nutmeg

¹/₂ teaspoon ground coriander

2 tablespoons distilled white vinegar

Kitchen Note: Chop meat and fat into 1-inch chunks, or the size indicated by the instructions for your sausage maker.

1. Process meat and fat through a sausage maker fitted with the large grinder attachment, following manufacturer's instructions.

2. In a large bowl, gently mix ground meat with salt, pepper, cloves, allspice, nutmeg, coriander, and vinegar until evenly distributed. Take care not to mash or tear apart the chunks of meat and fat.

3. Attach wet casing to the tubing attachment of the sausage maker. Tie a knot in the other end and poke a small hole at the end to release air.

4. Feed meat mixture through sausage maker into casing, following manufacturer's instructions, letting it create a coil. Leave a few inches of unfilled casing before cutting it from the machine. Knot the open end of the coil.

5. Wrap coil in parchment paper and store in an airtight container in the refrigerator for up to 4 days, or in the freezer for up to 3 months. Before serving, cook fully using one of the cooking methods beginning on page 15.

CONDIMENTS, SAUCES, AND TOPPINGS

What's better than homemade bread and sausage?
Homemade condiments! Most are so simple to prepare, you'll
wonder why you waited so long to whip them up yourself.

BARBECUE SAUCES

There are four general styles of barbecue sauce in the southern United States: Carolina, Memphis, Kansas City, and Texas. Countless Carolina-style sauces exist, but the best known is South Carolina's thick, sweet, tangy mustard-based version. Kansas City–style is a tomato-based sauce, often made with molasses and vinegar. Where the signature distinction of Memphis-style barbecue is dry-rub cooking, this style of barbecue features a sauce that is tomato based but less sweet and tangy than Kansas City's. Texas barbecue sauce, or Texas mop sauce, is the thinnest of the four and also not as sweet as the Kansas City variety; some Texas sauces are smoky and spicy, reflecting the influence of the state's neighbor to the south, Mexico. You can find all four styles in stores or make them at home. For an authentic alternative, find a well-known regional restaurant and see if you can buy their sauce (many now sell them nationally).

TEXAS BBQ SAUCE

Here's how we make the barbecue sauce in my home state. Usually served on the side rather than on the meat, this thin sauce can be used for dipping, topping, or as a mop sauce (brushed onto the meat throughout cooking to flavor it and keep it moist—so named because in large barbecue restaurants it is applied with an oversized brush that resembles a mop). I know I'm going to make a lot of barbecue fanatics unhappy by including a Texas barbecue sauce first . . . but it's the only kind I'll eat, and it's perfect for topping hot dogs.

MAKES ABOUT 1 QUART

3 cups water
1 cup ketchup
2 tablespoons distilled white vinegar
$1/4$ large white onion, grated
2 garlic cloves, finely chopped
2 teaspoons sugar
1 teaspoon molasses
1 tablespoon lemon juice
2 tablespoons Worcestershire sauce
1 teaspoon ground cumin
1 teaspoon ground paprika
$1/2$ teaspoon freshly ground black pepper
$1/2$ teaspoon ground chipotle pepper
$1/4$ teaspoon ground cayenne pepper

Combine all ingredients in a medium heavy-bottomed pot. Bring to a gentle simmer and cook for 30 minutes, until flavors have melded. Store in the refrigerator for up to a week. Serve warm or cool.

KANSAS CITY BBQ SAUCE

Sweeter and with more tomato flavor than Texas-style sauce, Kansas City's version is also less spicy and much thicker. Despite not being Texan, it's still delicious.

MAKES ABOUT 3 CUPS

2 cups ketchup
1/4 white onion, grated
2 garlic cloves, finely chopped
1/2 cup brown sugar
1/3 cup distilled white vinegar
2 tablespoons Worcestershire sauce
2 tablespoons yellow mustard
1 tablespoon molasses
1/2 teaspoon freshly ground black pepper
1/4 teaspoon ground cayenne pepper

Combine all ingredients in a medium heavy-bottomed pot. Bring to a gentle simmer and cook for 30 minutes, until flavors have melded. Store in an airtight container in the fridge for up to a week.

CAROLINA-STYLE BBQ SAUCE: Replace 1 cup ketchup with 1 cup yellow mustard. Eighty-six the onion, Worcestershire sauce, and molasses.

MEMPHIS-STYLE BBQ SAUCE: Double the vinegar and halve the brown sugar.

KETCHUPS

This tangy tomato-based condiment has been around for years in myriad varieties. There are two recipes that come together quickly. Note that you can add just about any flavoring or spice to make it your own.

QUICK KETCHUP

Just a few ingredients, and an equally minimal time commitment, produce a great-tasting homemade version of the store-bought favorite.

MAKES 2 CUPS

1 (16 ounce) can tomato sauce
1 (6 ounce) can tomato paste
2 tablespoons distilled white vinegar
$^{1}/_{4}$ cup sugar
1 whole clove
$^{1}/_{8}$ teaspoon ground cayenne pepper
$^{1}/_{4}$ teaspoon powdered garlic
$^{1}/_{4}$ teaspoon powdered onion

1. In a heavy-bottomed pot, stir to combine all ingredients. Bring to a simmer over medium-low heat, reduce heat to low, and cook for 1 hour, stirring occasionally.

2. Remove and discard clove. Transfer mixture to the bowl of a food processor and process until smooth. Store in the refrigerator for up to 2 weeks.

> **SPICY KETCHUP:** Increase the cayenne to $^{1}/_{2}$ teaspoon and add a few dashes of your favorite hot sauce.

> **SOUTH AFRICAN TOMATO SAUCE:** Add 1 (16-ounce) can stewed tomatoes with their juices at the same time as the tomato sauce and paste. Add 1 teaspoon cumin, $^{1}/_{2}$ teaspoon allspice, and $^{1}/_{2}$ teaspoon nutmeg with the spices.

BANANA KETCHUP

Banana ketchup is a popular condiment in the Philippines. It was invented during World War II in response to a shortage of tomatoes and has been enjoyed ever since. It's quite different from tomato ketchup, and it's easy to make at home.

MAKES ABOUT 1 CUP

1 tablespoon extra-virgin olive oil
$^{1}/_{4}$ large white onion, finely chopped
$^{1}/_{2}$ garlic clove, finely chopped
1 cup bananas, pureed or mashed
2 tablespoons distilled white vinegar
$^{1}/_{4}$ cup sugar
$^{1}/_{2}$ teaspoon ground cinnamon
$^{1}/_{4}$ teaspoon ground allspice
$^{1}/_{8}$ teaspoon ground cayenne pepper

1. In a heavy-bottomed pot, warm olive oil over medium-low heat. Add onions and garlic. Cover and cook for 20 minutes.

2. Add bananas, vinegar, sugar, cinnamon, allspice, and cayenne. Stir until evenly combined. Bring to a simmer, reduce heat to low, and cook for 20 minutes, stirring occasionally.

3. Transfer mixture to the bowl of a food processor and process until smooth. Store in the refrigerator for up to 4 days.

MAYONNAISES

Mayo is an emulsion, which means it's a combination of two ingredients that don't normally mix well. It requires an emulsifier (mostly egg, along with mustard for good measure), plus patience and a *lot* of whisking using one of these three methods.

BOWL AND WHISK: The best way to make mayonnaise is to enlist a friend to hold the mixing bowl and pour the oil so you can focus on whisking. If that's not an option, try placing a nonslip placemat or a wet dishtowel under the bowl to keep it from moving while you whisk.

STAND MIXER OR FOOD PROCESSOR: Using a food processor or stand mixer fitted with the whisk attachment will save you from feeling like your arm is going to fall off. Set the stand mixer to whip on high speed or run the food processor continuously while you pour the oil very slowly.

STICK BLENDER (IMMERSION BLENDER): This helpful tool blends and purees food in the same container you're already using. There's no need to whisk like crazy—or even clean an extra bowl. Slowly add the oil while keeping the whirring head of the blender in the egg mixture.

MAYONNAISE

Mayo is not something you often find on hot dogs in the United States, but it's a favorite condiment in many other parts of the world.

MAKES ABOUT 1 CUP

1 large egg yolk
$1/2$ teaspoon salt
$1/4$ teaspoon ground mustard
$1/8$ teaspoon onion powder
$1/8$ teaspoon garlic powder
$1/8$ teaspoon sugar
$1 1/2$ tablespoons distilled white vinegar
$3/4$ cup soybean oil

1. In a medium bowl, whisk together egg yolk, salt, ground mustard, onion powder, garlic powder, and sugar. Add vinegar and whisk until thoroughly combined.

2. While whisking continuously, add oil slowly, a couple drops a time. Whisk until all the oil has been added and the mayonnaise is thick.

> **WASABI MAYONNAISE:** Replace the onion powder and garlic powder with $1/2$ teaspoon wasabi powder.
>
> **VEGAN MAYONNAISE:** Combine 1 tablespoon finely ground flaxseed with 3 tablespoons water. Stir and set aside until mixture thickens, about 5 minutes. Prepare mayonnaise as instructed, replacing the egg yolk with 1 tablespoon of the flaxseed paste.

PICKLE MAYONNAISE (GURKMAJONNÄS)

Gurkmajonnäs literally translates as "cucumber mayonnaise." A popular condiment in Sweden, it is made with mayonnaise and pickled cucumber or relish. It's typically served on potatoes or sausage, and you can find it in the Swedish thin-bread roll, also known as *tunnbrödsrulle* (page 106).

MAKES ABOUT 1¹/₂ CUPS

1 cup sour cream
¹/₂ cup mayonnaise
¹/₄ cup chopped cucumber pickles
¹/₂ large white onion, chopped
1 teaspoon yellow mustard
Salt and pepper, to taste

Mix all ingredients together in a bowl. Serve immediately or store in an airtight container in the refrigerator for up to a week.

MUSTARDS

Although less contentious than ketchup, mustard on a hot dog can begin to become bewildering when you realize just how many varieties of mustard exist (the hot dog recipes in this book call for at least half a dozen). Nevertheless, mustard is simple to make and far less time-consuming than ketchup. It may not be any more economical than buying a commercial brand, but making your own gives you control over the ingredients (goodbye, artificial flavors and hard-to-pronounce chemical preservatives!), plus you can tailor the flavor to your liking.

More Mustard: The National Mustard Museum in Middleton, Wisconsin, began as a humble condiment collection in 1986. Today, it boasts over 5,500 mustards and countless items of mustard memorabilia (including spirit gear for the alma mater of mustard, Poupon U).

YELLOW MUSTARD

Homemade mustard looks and tastes like the real thing. The best part is that you can adjust the seasonings to your preference.

MAKES ³/₄ CUP

¹/₄ **cup ground mustard**
¹/₄ **cup distilled white vinegar**
3 tablespoons water
¹/₂ **teaspoon cornstarch**
1 teaspoon ground turmeric
¹/₈ **teaspoon cayenne pepper**
¹/₄ **teaspoon salt**
¹/₂ **teaspoon sugar**
Pinch garlic powder

Combine all ingredients in a small heavy-bottomed pot. Stirring constantly, bring mixture to a boil and then remove from heat. Store in an airtight container in the refrigerator for up to 1 week.

SPICY YELLOW MUSTARD: Double the cayenne pepper and add a dash of your favorite hot sauce.

DIJON MUSTARD: Substitute white wine vinegar for the vinegar and white wine for the water. Eighty-six the turmeric; add a pinch each of paprika and cayenne instead.

HORSERADISH MUSTARD: Add ¹/₄ teaspoon finely ground or grated horseradish root.

WHOLE GRAIN MUSTARD

If yellow mustard is too boring for you, try this version packed with tangy whole mustard seeds. This is a perfect topping for hearty hot dogs like those made with a fresh bratwurst.

MAKES ³/₄ CUP

2 tablespoons whole yellow mustard seeds
2 tablespoons whole brown mustard seeds
2 tablespoons white wine vinegar
2 tablespoons white wine
¹/₂ **teaspoon salt**
Pinch garlic powder

Break up three-fourths of the mustard seeds in a spice grinder or with a mortar and pestle. Combine with the whole seeds and remaining ingredients. Store in an airtight container in the refrigerator for up to a week.

BROWN (DELI) MUSTARD: Grind mustard seeds until very fine and add ¹/₄ teaspoon cayenne pepper, ¹/₄ teaspoon black pepper, and a dash of your favorite hot sauce with the other ingredients.

SPICY BROWN MUSTARD: Prepare brown mustard as instructed, but double the cayenne and hot sauce.

MISCELLANEOUS TOPPINGS

You won't find any inedible garnishes here. Load up on tasty trimmings for flavor-packed frankfurters.

SPICY AJÍ SAUCE

Ají is a popular South American sauce with origins in Peru. It is deliciously sweet and mild.

MAKES ABOUT 1 CUP

4 green chiles, such as jalapeños
3 green onions, white and light green parts only, chopped
$^1/_2$ small white onion, chopped
Leaves from 1 small bunch cilantro
Juice of 1 lime
$^1/_2$ teaspoon salt
$^1/_2$ teaspoon freshly ground black pepper

Combine all ingredients in a food processor and puree until smooth. Store in an airtight container in the refrigerator for up to a week.

COLESLAW

If you live in the South, you know what really good coleslaw is: creamy, packed with delicious veggies, and full of flavor.

MAKES ABOUT 1 QUART, ENOUGH FOR 8 HOT DOGS

$^1/_2$ head green cabbage, shredded
1 large carrot, grated
$^1/_2$ red onion, grated
$^1/_4$ cup mayonnaise
$^1/_4$ cup buttermilk
1 tablespoon sour cream
1 tablespoon sugar
$^1/_2$ teaspoon celery salt
$^1/_2$ teaspoon salt
$^1/_4$ teaspoon freshly ground black pepper

Thoroughly combine all ingredients in a large bowl. Refrigerate for at least 1 hour to allow flavors to blend. Store in an airtight container in the refrigerator for up to 3 days.

KATSU SAUCE

Although this sauce is easily found in many grocery stores, it's a snap to make at home.

$^1/_2$ cup ketchup
$^1/_2$ cup Worcestershire sauce
$^1/_4$ cup soy sauce
2 tablespoons molasses
1 tablespoon prepared mustard

Mix ingredients together until evenly blended.

CLASSIC HOT DOG CHILI

Everywhere you look, chili is topping hot dogs, and it seems that no two are exactly the same. Below is a no-frills version that's a solid template for any of the half dozen variations found in this book: a few simple changes, and you've got a Greek sauce, a Rochester meat sauce, or a spicy southwest chili.

**MAKES ABOUT 1 QUART,
ENOUGH FOR 4 HOT DOGS**

**2 tablespoons extra virgin olive oil
1 large white onion, diced
4 cloves garlic, finely chopped
1 teaspoon salt
$^1/_4$ teaspoon freshly ground black pepper
1 tablespoon ground chili powder
1 teaspoon ground cumin
$^1/_8$ teaspoon ground cayenne pepper
1 pound ground beef
1 cup beef stock
8 ounces tomato paste**

1. Heat olive oil in a large skillet over medium-high heat. Add onions and cook until soft and translucent, about 8 minutes, stirring occasionally. Add garlic and cook for another 2 minutes, stirring occasionally.

2. Add salt, black pepper, chili powder, cumin, cayenne, and beef. Cook until beef is browned and no trace of pink remains.

3. Reduce heat to medium-low and add beef stock and tomato paste. Stir until evenly combined. Simmer for 30 minutes, stirring occasionally. Serve immediately or store in an airtight container in the refrigerator for up to 3 days.

GREEK SAUCE: Eighty-six the cumin and cayenne. Add 1 teaspoon finely chopped fresh oregano, 1 teaspoon cinnamon, $^1/_8$ teaspoon allspice, and 1 whole clove with the spices. Just before serving, remove and discard the clove and add 1 teaspoon finely chopped fresh basil.

CONEY ISLAND SAUCE: Eighty-six the cumin and cayenne. Add 1 tablespoon yellow mustard with the spices. Substitute 8 ounces tomato sauce for tomato paste.

TOMATO-BASED CHILI SAUCE: Add 1 16-ounce can stewed diced tomatoes and their juices or 2 diced large fresh tomatoes along with the tomato paste.

RHODE ISLAND CHILI: Add 1 teaspoon ground mustard, 1 teaspoon paprika, $^1/_2$ teaspoon celery salt, and $^1/_4$ teaspoon ground allspice with the spices.

ROCHESTER MEAT SAUCE: Add 1 tablespoon Worcestershire sauce, 1 tablespoon yellow mustard, and 1 teaspoon fresh oregano with the spices.

SPICY SOUTHWEST CHILI: Add a handful of chopped assorted dried chilies of your choice (try arbol, cascabel, chipotle, guajillo, or pasilla) with the onions. Double the chili powder and triple the cumin and cayenne and add 1 teaspoon chipotle powder with the spices.

SPICY BEAN CHILI: Double the chili powder and cayenne. Add 1 cup cooked beans and a few drops of your favorite hot sauce with the beef stock.

DISTRICT CHILI: Add 1 teaspoon ground mustard, 1 teaspoon ground coriander, 1 bay leaf, and 1 tablespoon white wine vinegar with the spices in step 2. Remove bay leaf before serving or storing.

CLASSIC FRIES

Few foods go with hot dogs better than fries (heck, few foods are better on hot dogs than fries). To make them yourself, you need only three ingredients.

MAKES ENOUGH FOR 4 HOT DOGS

2 pounds russet potatoes (do not peel)
1 quart vegetable or peanut oil
Salt, to taste

1. Cut potatoes lengthwise into slices about ¼ inch thick, and then cut slices into sticks about ¼ inch wide. This will give you long rectangles that are about ¼ inch square.

2. Soak potatoes in cold water for 20 minutes. Meanwhile, heat oil to 300°F in a large pot.

3. Transfer potatoes to a towel or paper towels and dry thoroughly. Cover a countertop, baking sheet, or serving platter with fresh paper towels.

4. Working in batches, add potatoes to pot (do not overcrowd) and fry for 5 to 8 minutes, until light golden and cooked through. Transfer fries to paper towels to drain while you cook the remaining potatoes.

5. When all potatoes have been fried, increase oil temperature to 375°F.

6. Just before serving, fry potatoes a second time, working in batches, until golden brown, about 2 to 4 minutes.

7. Return fries to paper towels. While they're still oily, sprinkle salt over the fries and toss to coat.

FRIED POTATO WEDGES

Larger than fries, potato wedges have a crisp browned exterior with an irresistible creamy interior.

2 tablespoons extra virgin olive oil
1 pound russet potatoes, cut into 1-inch wedges
Salt, to taste

MAKES 16 WEDGES,
ENOUGH FOR 4 HOT DOGS

1. Heat olive oil in a large skillet over medium heat. Add potatoes and cook on one side for about 10 minutes, or until starting to brown.

2. Flip potatoes and cook for another 10 minutes, or until browned.

3. Flip once more and cook another 10 minutes on the third side, or until browned all over.

4. Transfer potatoes to a paper towel to drain. Sprinkle with salt and serve immediately.

> **THICK-CUT FRIES:** Cut fries into ½-inch-thick rectangles. Increase first cooking time by a couple minutes, if needed, until potatoes are tender. Keep second cooking time the same.
>
> **FRÎTES:** Increase first cooking time by 2 to 5 minutes, or until the fries begin to brown. Keep second cooking time the same.
>
> **WASABI FRIES:** After second cooking, toss fries with 1 teaspoon wasabi powder as well as salt.

MANGO CHUTNEY

Chutneys, often used in and originating from Indian cuisine, are flavorful sauces that typically accompany a main dish. This one is a perfect topping for an Indian-inspired hot dog (page 124).

MAKES ABOUT 2 CUPS

¹/₄ cup vinegar
¹/₂ cup granulated sugar
¹/₂ cup brown sugar
¹/₂ teaspoon ground cinnamon
¹/₂ teaspoon ground ginger
³/₄ teaspoon ground allspice
¹/₂ teaspoon ground nutmeg
2 whole cloves
¹/₄ teaspoon salt
¹/₄ large white onion, finely chopped
1 clove garlic, finely chopped
¹/₄ cup raisins
¹/₄ cup golden raisins
2 cups sliced mango

1. In a pot, bring vinegar, sugars, spices, and salt to a boil. Reduce heat and cook at a low boil for 30 minutes, until thick.

2. Add onions, garlic, and raisins and boil for another 30 minutes.

3. Add sliced mango and boil for 30 minutes to 1 hour, until mango just begins to break down. Remove from heat and let cool before serving. You can pour the chutney into sterilized jars if you wish to store it; it keeps for up to 1 year.

CHILI NAM CHIM

Nam chim in Thai simply means "dipping sauce," and it's a widely used condiment with nearly infinite variations, all with subtle nuances that can change the direction of a dish. This version is spicy and perfect on a haute dog.

MAKES ABOUT ¹/₂ CUP

5 jalapeños, finely chopped
1 clove garlic, finely chopped
1 tablespoon freshly grated ginger
1 teaspoon ground coriander
1 teaspoon sugar
¹/₄ cup fish sauce
2 tablespoons lime juice

Kitchen Note: Fish sauce—also known as nam pla or nuoc mam—is a staple of Asian cooking made by fermenting small fish in brine. Find it in the international aisle of the supermarket or at Asian grocers.

Place jalapeños, garlic, ginger, coriander, and sugar in the bowl of a food processor. Process until smooth. Add fish sauce and lime juice. Process until thoroughly combined. Store in an airtight container in the fridge for up to a few days.

NEW YORK STYLE SAUTÉED ONIONS

A few simple additions turn humble sautéed onions into an unexpected, tasty topping. Put them on your New York dog for an authentic taste of the Big Apple.

MAKES ABOUT 2 CUPS

2 tablespoons extra virgin olive oil
2 large white onions, sliced
2 tablespoons tomato paste
$1/8$ teaspoon ground cayenne pepper
$1/8$ teaspoon ground cinnamon

Warm olive oil in a skillet over medium-high heat. Cook onions with tomato paste and spices, stirring, until soft, translucent, and starting to brown on the edges, about 10 to 15 minutes. Serve immediately or store in an airtight container in the refrigerator for up to 3 days.

THE QUARTER-MILLION-DOLLAR DOG STAND

The cost of operating a hot dog cart near the Central Park Zoo? A cool $289,500 in license fees to the city of New York. At $2 a dog, breaking even means feeding a lot of mouths.

CRUNCHY FRIED ONIONS

If I have a guilty pleasure—aside from eating hot dogs 24/7, that is—it is snacking on these. I can't seem to get enough of their irresistible texture and flavor. They're as delicious on any hot dog as they are out of hand.

ABOUT 1 CUP, ENOUGH FOR 4 DOGS

2 quarts vegetable oil
1 large yellow onion, thinly sliced
1 cup milk
1 egg
1 cup flour
1 tablespoon salt
$1/2$ tablespoon freshly ground black pepper

1. Heat oil in a large pot to 375°F.

2. Combine milk and egg in a bowl. In another bowl, combine flour, salt, and black pepper.

3. Working in batches, dip onions in milk mixture to coat and then dip them straight in flour mixture to coat. Transfer to a plate until all the onions are coated.

4. Again working in batches, place a handful or two of battered onions in the hot oil. Cook for 2 to 5 minutes, or until golden brown. Transfer to a paper towel to drain.

GUACAMOLE

Guacamole may be the king of all condiments, at least for us Southerners who are lucky enough to live in the Tex-Mex region. We add guacamole (and melted cheese) to everything. Spicy Mexican dishes aside, guacamole is a great way to freshen up a hot dog, adding a delicious avocado bite to your favorite wiener.

MAKES ABOUT 2 CUPS

4 or 5 ripe avocados
1 medium tomato, diced
1 small white onion, finely chopped
2 cloves garlic, diced
Leaves from 1 small bunch cilantro
Juice of 1 lime
Salt and pepper, to taste

1. Scoop avocado flesh into a medium bowl; discard pit and skins. Using a fork, mash to the desired consistency. It can be as chunky or smooth as you like.

2. Add tomatoes, onions, garlic, cilantro, and lime juice. Stir to combine and add salt and pepper to taste.

3. Serve immediately or refrigerate in an airtight container for up to 1 day.

SHRIMP SALAD

Of all the sides, toppings, and condiments found on hot dogs, this is likely the most surprising. I can't say shrimp salad is delicious on all hot dogs, but it's a staple for an authentic Swedish *tunnbrödsrulle* (see page 106).

MAKES ABOUT 1 CUP

2 teaspoons olive oil
1/2 pound fresh shrimp, peeled and deveined
1/4 cup mayonnaise
1 tablespoon spicy brown mustard
1 tablespoon ketchup
1/2 teaspoon salt
1/4 teaspoon freshly ground pepper

1. Heat oil in a large skillet over medium-low heat.

2. Add shrimp and cook for 2 to 5 minutes on each side, or until shrimp is pink and cooked through. Remove from the pan and let cool.

3. Combine cooled shrimp in a large bowl with mayonnaise, mustard, ketchup, salt, and pepper. Serve immediately or store in the refrigerator for up to 2 days.

PULLED PORK

Although pulled pork can be an entire meal in itself, it also happens to be a delicious hot dog topping. Perfect for any barbecue-style dog, this pulled pork is moist and flavorful.

MAKES 2 TO 3 POUNDS

Oak wood chips, for grilling
4 pounds bone-in trimmed pork butt
¼ cup vegetable oil
¼ to ½ cup Texas Dry Rub (store-bought or from scratch, right)

1. Soak wood chips in water for 1 hour. Meanwhile, rub pork with oil, followed by a generous amount of Texas dry rub. Let sit covered at room temperature for 1 hour, or until meat comes to room temperature.

2. Preheat a grill or smoker to 275°F. If using a grill, heat only one side; cooking the pork with indirect heat will keep it from cooking too quickly. Place pork directly on the grate on the unheated side of the grill, or high in the smoker. Place soaked wood chips in a pan on the heated side of the grill, or place them in the wood chip tray of the smoker. Cook for 6 hours, or until the meat's internal temperature reaches 180°F.

3. Remove pork from heat and let rest at room temperature for about 30 minutes, or until cool enough to handle. Pull apart meat with a fork or, if you're brave, your bare hands.

TEXAS DRY RUB

If you're going to make Texas barbecue, you're going to need a Texas dry rub. This blend of spices is the definitive aspect of the style of barbecue native to the Lone Star State, and it's great for pulled pork, brisket, and just about any barbecue dog you can imagine. Try sprinkling these spices on your favorite hot dog to give it a spicy bite.

MAKES ½ CUP, ENOUGH TO SEASON 2 TO 4 POUNDS OF MEAT

¼ cup salt
2 tablespoons freshly ground black pepper
1 tablespoon ground cumin
1 teaspoon ground mustard
1 teaspoon ground chili powder
½ teaspoon ground cayenne pepper

Stir to combine all ingredients in a small bowl. Store in an airtight container for up to 2 months.

RÉMOULADE

Rémoulade is a French mayonnaise-based condiment similar to tartar sauce that adds a creamy tang to hot dogs.

MAKES ABOUT 1 CUP

¾ **cup mayonnaise (store-bought or from scratch, page 149)**
1 **teaspoon yellow mustard**
½ **small white onion, finely chopped**
1 **small kosher pickle, finely chopped**
½ **teaspoon curry powder**
¼ **teaspoon salt**

Kitchen Note: For this recipe, homemade mayonnaise is more than worth the trouble—rémoulade lets its clear, bright flavors shine through. Experiment with additional mix-in ingredients, like finely chopped gherkins, herbs, anchovies, and capers.

Stir to combine all ingredients. Cover and refrigerate for at least 15 minutes to let the flavors meld. Store in an airtight container in the refrigerator for up to 3 days. Serve chilled.

SALSA GOLF

Legend has it that this thick, creamy dipping sauce was invented by Nobel Prize–winning chemist Luis Federico Leloir at a seaside golf resort in his native Argentina. Bored with dipping shrimp in mayo, he grabbed ketchup and mayonnaise and mixed up this tangy sauce. It's the perfect companion for shrimp, scallops, salads, and—of course—haute dogs.

MAKES ABOUT 1 CUP

½ **cup mayonnaise**
½ **cup ketchup**
1 **teaspoon hot sauce**
¼ **teaspoon salt**
¼ **teaspoon black pepper**

Kitchen Notes: Homemade mayo and ketchup aren't a necessity, but they make this sauce special. For recipes, see pages 148-149. Try swapping the ketchup for barbecue sauce, or adding garlic, chiles, or other herbs and spices

Stir to combine all ingredients. Cover and refrigerate for at least 15 minutes and up to 2 weeks. Serve chilled.

Today, Salsa Golf (literally, "golf sauce") and similar recipes are enjoyed across South America and around the world. You may know it as fry sauce (mainly in Utah and Idaho), *rosé sauce* (Brazil), *mayoketchup* (Puerto Rico), *ketchup-mayo* (France), *cocktailsaus* (Belgium), *salsa rosa* (Spain), or Marie Rose sauce (United Kingdom). Commercial varieties are available locally and online, most notably Some Dude's Fry Sauce, a brand based in Salt Lake City, Utah.

SALSA VERDE

Salsa verde is a green salsa made using tomatillos, a small green fruit similar to a tomato. It has a deliciously fresh flavor, and in addition to making a great hot dog topping, it's a perfect salsa for chips. Give it a try on any of your favorite American dogs for an extra kick.

MAKES ABOUT 2 CUPS

1 pound tomatillos, skinned and halved
2 medium tomatoes, quartered
1 small white onion, quartered
$^1/_2$ small jalapeño, seeded
4 cloves garlic, finely chopped
Juice of 1 lime
1 teaspoon ground cumin
$^1/_4$ teaspoon ground cayenne pepper
Salt and pepper, to taste

Kitchen Note: Tomatillos are juicy green fruits in the nightshade family that resemble tomatoes. Thanks to their tart, fresh flavor and silky smooth texture, they are a key ingredient in salsas, sauces, and other elements of Mexican and Central American cuisine.

1. Preheat the oven to 400°F. Place tomatillos, tomatoes, onions, and jalapeños on a baking sheet and roast for 15 to 20 minutes, or until they begin to brown around the edges.

2. Place roasted vegetables in the bowl of a food processor. Add remaining ingredients and process until vegetables are broken up but still slightly chunky.

3. Let salsa cool before serving. Store in an airtight container in the refrigerator for up to 1 week.

VINAIGRETTE

This dressing isn't restricted to just salads anymore. You can find this tangy sweet sauce on hot dogs all across the globe.

MAKES ABOUT 1 CUP

$^3/_4$ cup extra virgin olive oil
$^1/_4$ cup apple cider vinegar
$^1/_4$ teaspoon salt
$^1/_4$ teaspoon freshly ground black pepper

In a bowl, whisk together all ingredients. Serve immediately or store in an airtight container in the refrigerator for up to a week.

ARUGULA PESTO

Traditional pesto is made with basil, pine nuts, garlic, oil, and Parmesan cheese. This version, made with peppery arugula, will give your favorite hot dogs a fresh bite.

MAKES ABOUT 2 CUPS

1 cup arugula leaves
$^1/_4$ large white onion, diced
2 cloves garlic, minced
$^1/_2$ cup pine nuts
$^1/_2$ cup shredded Parmesan cheese
$^1/_2$ teaspoon salt
$^1/_2$ teaspoon freshly ground black pepper
$^1/_2$ cup olive oil

Place arugula, onions, garlic, pine nuts, cheese, salt, and pepper in the bowl of a food processor. Process until mixture is smooth and ingredients are evenly distributed. With processor running, slowly pour in oil until mixture is smooth and creamy. Use immediately or store in the refrigerator for up to a week.

RELISH

If you like relish, you'll love this easy homemade version. In fact, you'll probably find yourself spreading it on more than just hot dogs.

MAKES 2 CUPS

About 4 small cucumbers (8 ounces), roughly chopped
About $1/4$ large onion (2 ounces), roughly chopped
1 tablespoon salt
$1/2$ cup distilled white vinegar
$1/2$ tablespoon sugar
8 whole peppercorns
1 whole clove
1 teaspoon whole mustard seeds
1 teaspoon ground coriander
Pinch ground cayenne pepper

1. Process cucumber and onion in a food processor until very fine. Transfer mixture to a small bowl, stir in salt, and refrigerate, covered, for 24 hours.

2. Remove bowl from fridge; drain and discard liquid. Set vegetables aside.

3. In a small heavy-bottomed pot, bring remaining ingredients to a boil. Boil for about 10 minutes, until liquid has reduced by one-quarter.

4. Strain and discard peppercorns, clove, and mustard seeds. Pour liquid over vegetables and toss to coat. Store in an airtight container in the refrigerator for up to 1 week.

NEON-GREEN RELISH: After adding the liquid in step 4, add a few drops of bright green food coloring.

CHILI RELISH: Halve the cucumber and onion. In step 1, add $1/4$ large (1-ounce) red bell pepper, $1/4$ large (1-ounce) yellow bell pepper, 1/2 large (1-ounce) jalapeño, $1/4$ large (1-ounce) poblano pepper, and $1/2$ large ($1/2$-ounce) serrano pepper, all roughly chopped. For a milder relish, use more bell pepper; if you like things hot, increase the amounts of jalapeños, poblanos, and/or serranos.

PINEAPPLE RELISH

Any classic relish lover will want to try this sweet and tangy take on the popular hot dog condiment. It's bright and juicy from the pineapple, zingy thanks to the ginger, and even a little bit spicy from the jalapeño.

MAKES ABOUT 1 CUP

$3/4$ cup pineapple, fresh and finely chopped or from 1 can crushed
2 tablespoons finely chopped red onion
1 jalapeño, seeded and finely chopped
1 teaspoon peeled and grated fresh ginger
Juice of 1 lime
$1/4$ teaspoon salt
$1/4$ teaspoon freshly ground black pepper

In a medium bowl, stir together all ingredients. Store in an airtight container in the refrigerator for up to 3 days.

SOURCES

For mail-order hot dogs, meat, casings, and meat sauces, as well as curing, smoking, and cooking supplies:

Glazier's Hot Dogs (uncured, neon red, pork and veal, and other hard-to-find varieties): shop.glazierhotdog.com

Heritage Foods USA: heritagefoodsusa.com

IKEA's Swedish Food Market (Swedish and Scandinavian sausages): ikea.com

Koegel's: koegelmeats.com

The Meat Hook: the-meathook.com

Nathan's: nathansfamous.com

Oscar Mayer: kraftbrands.com/oscarmayer

Paradise Locker Meats: paradisemeats.com

Sabrett's: sabrett.com

Scandinavian Kitchen: scandikitchen.co.uk

Vienna Beef: viennabeef.com

For vegan Italian sausage, veggie dogs, and soy and tofu dogs:

Morningstar Farms: morningstarfarms.com

Soy Boy Not Dogs, Franks, and Links: soyboy.com

Tofurkey Dogs and Links: tofurkey.com

Trader Joe's: traderjoes.com

Veggie Patch: veggiepatch.com

Worthington Leanies: worthingtonfoods.com

Wegmans: wegmans.com

Whole Foods: wholefoods.com

For sausage making and hot dog cooking equipment, visit eBay and Amazon as well as these independent shops:

Allied Kenco Sales: alliedkenco.com

Brooklyn Kitchen: thebrooklynkitchen.com

Butcher Packer: butcher-packer.com

Davison's Butcher Supply: davisonsbutcher.com

Emilio Miti: emiliomiti.com

LEM Products: lemproducts.com

Natural Casing Company: naturalcasingco.com

The Sausage Maker: sausagemaker.com

Weston Supply: westonsupply.com

For condiments, sauces, spices, and specialty foods—everything from sriracha and katsu sauce to Sabrett's signature Sautéed Onion Sauce:

Central Market (domestic and imported foods): Centralmarket.com

French's: frenchs.com

Glusto's: glustos.com

Gulden's: conagrafoods.com

H-E-B (Texas and Mexico): heb.com

H Mart (Korean): hmart.com

Heinz: Heinz.com

Hong Kong Supermarket (Chinese and Pan-Asian): hk2-district.com

IKEA's Swedish Food Market (Swedish and Scandinavian food): ikea.com

Inglehoffer: beavertonfoods.com

Mitsuwa Marketplace (Japanese): mitsuwa.com/english

Rancho Gordo: ranchogordo.com

Sabrett's: sabrett.com

Scandinavian Kitchen: scandikitchen.co.uk

Whole Foods: wholefoods.com

Whole Spice: wholespice.com

Wine Forest Wild Foods: wineforest.com

Woeber's Sweet Hot Mister Mustard (and other varieties): woebermustard.com

ACKNOWLEDGMENTS

Since I've forced a lot of people to dedicate their lives to hot dogs whilst writing this book, I should probably thank them.

I must of course thank my friends and family who began to dread asking, "What are we eating?" about two months in to this book. "Hot dogs. We're eating hot dogs again. And you'll like it," became my standard reply. You can probably see why they get to be on this page now.

Most important, though, are all the geniuses at Quirk who managed to turn the inane ramblings of a hot dog obsessed boy into the beautiful cookbook you are now holding. First, thank you to my editor, Margaret McGuire, for tolerating my impressive ability to miss every deadline, and more impressive penchant for misspelling every word known to man. A special thanks goes to copy editor Jane Morley for doing whatever copy editing is—my guess is fixing all my misspellings. Another special thanks to Amanda Richmond for designing this gorgeous book. And last but not least Nicole De Jackmo, Eric Smith, and the rest of the Quirk team. I am grateful to all who had their hands in this project and helped create what has been the most fun, delicious, and, albeit not the healthiest, certainly most worthwhile project I have ever been a part of.

INDEX

HUNGRY FOR MORE?

Hit up QuirkBooks.com/HauteDogs to download an exclusive recipe card, discover the best beverage pairings for each haute dog, pin and share your creations, and read an exclusive interview with the author. *Bon appétit!*